Catfish at the Pump
Humor and the Frontier

Catfish at the Pump
Humor and the Frontier

"There is no more dangerous literary symptom than a temptation to write about wit and humor. It indicates a total loss of both."

—George Bernard Shaw

University of Nebraska Press
Lincoln and London

First Bison Book printing: 1986
Most recent printing indicated by the first digit below:
  2 3 4 5 6 7 8 9 10

Library of Congress Cataloging-in-Publication Data
Welsch, Roger L.
   Catfish at the pump.
   Reprint. Originally published: Lincoln, Neb.:
Plains Heritage, c1982.
   Includes bibliographical references.
   1. American wit and humor—West (U.S.)—History and
criticism. 2. American literature—West (U.S.)—History
and criticism. 3. West (U.S.) in literature.
4. Frontier and pioneer life in literature. 5. Tall
tales—History and criticism. I. Welsch, Linda K.
II. Title.
PS430.W4 1986   817'.009'3278   86-4295
ISBN 0-8032-4740-0
ISBN 0-8032-9712-2 (pbk.)

Reprinted by arrangement with Roger L. Welsch

Copyrighted passages from Merrill Mattes's *The Great Platte River Road* and from the *Nebraska History* magazine are used by permission of Marvin Kivett, director, Nebraska State Historical Society.

Copyrighted passages from Robert Athearn's *High Country Empire* (1960) are used by permission of the University of Nebraska Press and the author.

Copyrighted materials from *The Gentle Tamers* © 1958 by Dee Brown reprinted by permission of Literistic, Ltd., and the author.

Copyrighted passages from Stan Hoig's *The Humor of the American Cowboy* (1958) are used by permission of the author.

Copyrighted passages from *The Great Plains* by Walter Prescott Webb, © Copyright, 1931, by Walter Prescott Webb. Used by permission of the publisher, Ginn and Company (Xerox Corporation).

∞

For my Father

TABLE OF CONTENTS

FOREWORD AND INTRODUCTION:

Despite the unforgiveably bad timing of publishing a book of lies during an election year when any novelty of the subject is out of the question, I was delighted with the reception given *Shingling the Fog and Other Plains Lies* (Swallow, 1972; University of Nebraska, 1980), my first effort to deal with pioneer humor. A good many people other than my mother thought the book was informative as well as amusing, and heaven knows, I enjoyed working with the materials. In fact, in reading the proofs I found it hard to keep my mind on the task of looking for words like "Sandhiils" or "peice" because I was instead *reading* the book and laughing at the stories. That may sound shamefully like laughing at one's own jokes but that is not at all the case. The jokes are not mine; I am not even a good storyteller. I have only been fortunate enough to be entrusted with them by their true owners, the storytellers, to pass along to you.

Once again I have become the caretaker of such a treasure trove. It is not the same kind of material that appeared in *Shingling the Fog*, however. In that volume I used primarily tall tales which I collected from oral sources or that were transmitted to me by the tellers; secondarily, stories previously recorded from folk sources in newspapers or folklore publications; and finally a few items that appear to be traditional but which were found in literary sources, particularly Mark Twain and Mari Sandoz. Some of the materials that appear on these pages are of the same nature—stories told me over a glass of beer, served up as retorts at the foot of a podium from which I had just delivered a series of these tales, or lies recorded in other studies of Plains pioneer life; but the backbone of the collection comes from the remarkable files of the Nebraska Federal Writers Project section of the Works Progress Administration, gleaned in turn from pioneer newspapers and oral sources.

During the worst and final years of the Great Depression jobs were created for the jobless, the benefits of which we enjoy in enormous degree yet today: park trails and facilities, dams, forests, monuments, and so forth. One section of this massive, admirable, still desperately needed effort was the Federal Writers Project, a program designed to give work to writers out of work. They were set to combing old newspaper files for historical and cultural data, assembling studies of ethnic communities, and developing the excellent Guide Book series for the states, a series that still stands as an unmatched classic today.

In Nebraska a good part of the writers' work was addressed to the collection of Plains folklore. It was intended that the pick of this material would eventually appear as a book or a set of books, and, indeed, a preliminary series of "Nebraska Folklore Pamphlets" did appear in mimeographed form from 1937 through 1940. But then World War II stopped everything in the United States that did not directly contribute to the struggle, and the Nebraska Federal Writers Project files were put into desk drawers, cabinets, and cardboard boxes that remained closed for some time.

In 1963 I used the mimeographed pamphlets, or at least a major part of them, to assemble *Treasury of Nebraska Pioneer Folklore* (University of Nebraska Press, 1966). I knew that the pamphlets contained only selections from the larger files and so I immediately began to look for the lost, complete file drawers. Tantalizing fragments were located in collections at the Library of Congress, but I also got depressing reports that minor officials and bureaucrats had pirated the collection upon the closing of the FWP offices.

With the help of Dr. C. Robert Keppel of the University of Omaha (now the University of Nebraska at Omaha) I found a major portion of the Omaha office's files in the basement of the University library, where they were residing after being moved in from beneath the seats of the football stadium. I spent many days separating the mouse-nibbled, bird-bedunged, scrambled mess and duplicating those parts that might be useful in folklore studies.

But once more the taste was only tantalizing: it was still clear that these were not the files I was looking for because very little of the materials I used in *Treasury of Nebraska Pioneer Folklore*, which we knew had been extracted from the major files, appeared in these musty papers.

I had pretty well given up the idea of ever finding the files when one day in a casual conversation John Demaris, a friend and former colleague at Nebraska Wesleyan University, remarked that he had been at a party the evening before where Jim Potter, the archivist at the Nebraska State Historical Society, had amused the guests by reading some pioneer tales he had found while sorting through some old WPA files.

That was a Sunday evening, and on Monday morning at 9:01 I was ringing Jim Potter's office telephone.

Mr. Potter led me to the materials I wanted and he was as helpful and generous with his time and knowledge as I have learned to expect the Nebraska State Historical Society staff to be. I found a good quantity of tall tales and other forms of frontier humor, recounted to a great extent in this book, as well as precious materials on other aspects of the Plains frontier.

There are certainly other files still buried in basements and under football bleachers elsewhere but for the moment I am exulting that I have finally found the tall-tale and humor collection, because these stories are what I have come to enjoy most of pioneer lore and which I am most anxious to share with others at this time in my work.

The central thesis of this volume is the same as it was in *Shingling the Fog and Other Plains Lies*: from these stories we learn something about the pioneers' attitudes, especially their attitudes toward the geography of the frontier lands between the mountains and toward the very nature of frontier living.

If at first we are surprised that frontiersmen involved in the unromantic, life-or-death job of homesteading found the strength and humor to laugh, it becomes very apparent upon talking with old-timers themselves that it was precisely this sense of humor in the face of incredible adversity that helped them find the courage necessary for survival. Robert Athearn, in *High Country Empire*, noted quite correctly,

> The frontiersman's traditional answer to adversity was humor. The plains farmer found that it helped him face new and desperate problems. When the land dried up, he laughed over the report that toll-bridge keepers were going broke because teamsters drove their animals across the trickling rivers right alongside the bridges. Or the story of the homesteader who wrote to a wire-fence company saying, "Send me your terms for fence wire. I am thinking of fencing in Kansas," to which the company gravely answered, "Have consulted the best authorities, and made an approximate calculation of the amount of wire it will take to fence in Kansas. We find that we have just enough if you order at once."
>
> Story after story . . . made the rounds of the west. The yarns were a candid admission of the difficulties to be faced, yet in their exaggeration they served to bolster the morale of those who endured times of tribulation. One observer of this spirit of exaggeration wrote, "In the West, it is all pervading; from cradle to deathbed, through sickness and adversity, it cheers the western man." And there was need of cheering. Thrust into a situation that was new, faced by forces that were larger than he had ever known before, the Westerner was scared. To laugh at the seriousness of the situation was his best answer to the problem. It was all he could do unless he wanted to quit.[1]

During the Winter of 1972 I heard a guest lecturer at the Geography Department of the University of Nebraska—a talented, intense young Easterner—announce solemnly that his study of 19th-century attitudes toward the Plains area during the frontier years was hampered by the lack of access to folk attitudes other than those expressed in diaries and accounts, semi-elitist forms. He had apparently forgotten or ignored the rich trove of songs and stories that have vividly recorded these attitudes. That they were valid is certified unmistakably by the fact that they persisted. If the songs and tales had not been significantly appropriate they

would not have been passed on, developed, nurtured, trea-
sured, repeated, collected—and published finally here.

Furthermore, we on the Plains are close enough to our
frontier history that when we need verification all we need
to do is seek out a frontiersman and ask him our question.
The ruts of the Oregon Trail are still to be seen, gouged out
of the Nebraska loess by hundreds of thousands of wheels;
the sod house, that more than any other single element
made possible the white settlement of the Plains, can be stud-
ied not only in archaeological excavations but in fact too,
for hundreds still stand, dozens are still lived in.[2] It has not
been long since the shadow of the frontier first fell on the
Plains.

So it is too with the pioneers who made the ruts and
built the soddies. I spent an afternoon several years ago
with a lady who recalled her memories of having been kid-
napped by a band of Indians and then being ransomed by
her father. On the other side of the coin, Richard Fool Bull,
a proud, 95-year-old Sioux, was once visiting my home. He
spoke with animation of his role in the occupation and siege
of Wounded Knee in the early 1970's. Then he played
some Lakota flute music for my children, and finally he
began talking about Wounded Knee again. He clapped his
hands rapidly to describe the sound of the guns—and I was
puzzled, because I was not aware that automatic weapons
had been used. "Were those the AK-47s that the Indians
had?" I asked. He looked at me, also puzzled. "No," he
said, "Those were the Hotchkiss guns." He was talking
about the *first* Wounded Knee, of 1890.

Even though some of the stories in the following collection are not old—some have been told to me during the
past week—they and their style are nonetheless age-old. The
tall tale and the jest are venerable, ancient forms, but they
do seem to have found their most fertile soil on the North
American continent. The planting of the genre was early. In
The Bear Went Over the Mountain[3] R. B. Downs says,

> The state of scientific knowledge and the credulous-
> ness of America's colonial ancestors are indicated further
> by an incident reported as fact by Cotton Mather in 1712

to the Royal Society of London. As printed in the Society's *Philosophical Transactions*, Mather wrote: "A Person
provoking a Rattle-Snake to bite the Edge of a broad Ax
he had in his Hand; the colour of the Steeled part bitten
was immediately changed, and at the first stroke he made
with it in using his Ax, the so discoloured part broke out,
leaving a gap in his Ax."

That is a story that persisted well into 20th-century
Nebraska and was also transferred to the mysterious—and
even more deadly—hoop snake.

The American propensity for inventing and telling
about such creatures has given him a reputation that may
have been bestowed with malice but which was and still is
born with pride. From *Harpers Weekly* of 1857[4] comes a
double entendre epitaph which the honoree most certainly
would have accepted with a modest blush and a proud
smile:

Here lies the tongue of Godfrey Lill,
Which always lied, and lies here still.

Joe Miller, whose 19th-century jokebook puts him in
the forefront of the proponents of and influences on American humor, recorded the nationalistic, regionalistic, chauvin-
istic, unabashed nature of the humor that he knew so
well:

A Kentuckian was once asked what he considered
the boundaries of the United States. "The boundaries of
our country, sir?" he replied. "Why sir, on the north we
are bounded by the Aurora Borealis, on the east we are
bounded by the rising sun, on the south we are bounded
by the procession of the Equinoxes, and on the west by
the Day of Judgement."[5]

And G. D. Prentiss, editor of the *Louisville Journal* during
the mid to late 19th century, provided an example of the
competitive nature that persisted within the tall-tale
tradition:

A western editor boasts that his State furnishes a
greater quantity of oats than any other in the Union. He
forgets to say whether she also furnished a greater
number of asses to eat them.

There was certainly a tall-tale tradition in Europe and England; that is always thrown into the face of people like me who deal with and dote on the American tall tale. But I tell you, Sir, that those tales from abroad must blush in comparison. It is the difference between the kiss of a sister and that of a lover.

More objective evidence of the disparity is provided by baffled Europeans and Englishmen themselves, and by the bemused Americans looking on. Rarely do the visitors express an understanding or appreciation of the American tall tale. Worse yet, a good proportion of their reports suggests that they not only did not "get" the jokes, but they didn't even know they were jokes. H. L. Mencken wrote that Fredrick Marryat, an English traveler, said he heard "one of the first men in America" say, "Sir, if I had done so, I should not only have doubled and trebled, but I should have fourbled and fivebled my money." Mencken notes, "Unfortunately, it is hard to believe that an American who was so plainly alive to the difference between shall and will, should and would, would have been unaware of quadrupled and quintupled. No doubt there was humor in the country, then as now, and visiting Englishmen were sometimes taken for rides."[6]

Marryat himself wrote in his *A Diary in America with Remarks on its Institutions* in 1836,

> I had a genuine Yankee story from one of the party on deck. I was inquiring if the Hudson was frozen up or not during the winter. This led to a conversation as to the severity of the winter, when one man, by way of proving how cold it was, said, "Why, I had a cow on my lot up the river and last winter she got in among the ice, and was carried down three miles before we could get her out again. The consequence has been that she has milked nothing but *ice creams* ever since."

Furthermore, Marryat also provides us with background material that shows that the American was laughing at himself a good deal more than he was laughing at anyone else:

> Progressing in the stage, I had a very amusing specimen of the ruling passion of the country—the spirit of

barter, which is communicated to the females as well as to the boys. I will stop for a moment, however, to say that I heard of an American who had two sons, and he declared that they were so clever at barter that he locked them both up together in a room, without a cent in their pockets, and that before they had *swopped* for an hour, they had each gained two dollars apiece.

Finally, a comment from one of the most observant of observing Americans, Josh Billings:

Amerikans luv caustic things; they would prefer turpentine to colone water, if they had to drink either. So with the relish of humour; they must hav it on the half-shell with cayenne. An Englishman wants his fun smothered deep in mint sauce, and he is willing tew wait till next day before he tastes it. If yu tickle or convince an Amerikan yu have got to do it quick. An Amerikan luvs to laff, but he don't luv to make a bizziness ov it; he works, eats, and hawhaws on a canter. I guess the English hav more wit, and the Amerikans more humour. We havn't had time yet to bile down our humour and get the wit out ov it.

To call the American frontiersman a "peasant" would have earned you a torn ear or gouged eye, but with the safety that comes from historical perspective, I'll declare him that, a peasant, at the same time more provincial and yet infamously more cosmopolitan than his European or English parallels. He revelled and delighted in his crudity and uncouthness. It was a banner that he flaunted on any and every occasion, to horrify the proper, to scandalize the prim, to deflate the pompous. When the bumpkin entered the refined home, he spit on the floor just as he did in his dirt-floored log or sod cabin. If the hostess tried to anticipate his aim by moving her brass cuspidor to his range, he warned her that if she didn't move that fancy chamberpot there was every chance in the world that he was going to wind up spitting into it.

It was his honesty matched up with the splendid pretense of "civilization":

Almost the only opportunity which the younger men had of seeing anything of the world beyond was when in the autumn a party would harness up their teams and carry their spare produce to the nearest town, some days' journey off. They would camp out at night, and as lucifer-matches had not yet reached them, they were obliged to trust for fire to a brand borrowed from the nearest house. Such a party once encamped near a fine dwelling, dispatched one of their number to borrow a brand. He was courteously received by the good lady, who made him sit down in a parlor furnished, to his view, most gorgeously, with a carpet and half a dozen Windsor chairs. When he returned he described his adventure to his companions:

"I tell you, boys—with my dirty britches I sot right smack in one o' the finest Weasler chairs you uver seen in all yer borned days, and my big, mud-bustin', piss-ant-killin' shoes on thar fine carpet looked like two great big Injun canoes. I'll be poxed ef I knowed how to hold my hands nur feet."[7]

The tall tale was one of the most popular and visible forms of humor on the frontier but it was certainly not the only form or even the most important one. It would be hard to establish any accurate hierarchy of that sort. The practical joke was in its heyday in 19th-century America, for example. On the Plains, cowboys were putting bull snakes in blanket rolls and burs under saddles while sod-busters at the square dances were wiring together front and back wagon wheels in the yard and pinning the babies in the upstairs bedroom to the quilt with safety pins.

Sometimes the jokes and pranks strike us more refined folks as sharp or even cruel but in the area of jests and tall tales I tend to agree with Josh Billings, who said,

"Enny man who can swop horses, or ketch fish, and not lie about it, is just about as pious az men ever get to in this world,"

and piety was held in notoriously low esteem on the frontier.

Nor were the lies ever meant to deceive. That was the secret and distinguishing characteristic of the tall tale—it was assumed that anyone with half a brain would know that they were lies. J. Frank Dobie understood more about

Western humor than anyone else and expressed that understanding brilliantly:

> An authentic liar knows what he is lying about, knows that his listeners—unless they are tenderfeet, greenhorns—know also, and hence makes no pretense of fooling either himself or them. At his best he is as grave as a historian of the Roman Empire; yet what he is after is neither credulity nor the establishment of truth. He does not take himself too seriously, but he does regard himself as an artist and yearns for recognition of his art. He may lie with satiric intent; he may lie merely to make the time pass pleasantly; he may lie in order to take the wind out of some egotistic fellow of his own tribe or to take in some greener; again, without any purpose at all and directed only by his ebullient and companion-loving nature, he may "stretch the blanket" merely because like the redoubtable Tom Ochiltree, he had "rather lie on credit than tell the truth for cash." His generous nature revolts at the monotony of everyday facts and overflows with desire to make his company joyful.[8]

Nineteenth-century frontier newspapers occupied a position that confounds the customary categories used by modern folklore scholars. Newspapers, we understand, are not the stuff of folklore but of popular culture. Folklore is transmitted by informal means—word of mouth, example, hand-written notes, that sort of thing; popular culture uses mass media for its transmission—television, radio, comic books, phonograph records, and newspapers.

But newspapers do sometimes even today publish folklore, sometimes as news, sometimes as folklore. And newspapers can be *reflections* of folklore too. Editors are, and were, not reluctant to borrow the folk phrase, the folk idea, the folk anecdote, and apply it to their own purposes.

In the 19th century the newspapers were of the folk. Editors might have been educated but above all they had the money and inclination to run a newspaper, the wit to write, and enough education to spell it.

On the Plains there were newspapers in nearly every village. Every village, after all, aspired to be the state capital eventually. Moreover, almost every village had two newspapers—one Republican, one Democratic; one Catholic, one Protestant; one dry, one wet; one Danish, one Polish; one interventionist, one isolationist; one trees-bring-the-rain, another plows-bring-the-rain. The cozy arrangements of "sister" publications were not the rule then. The language was rough and unrestrained. Editors let fire their best salvos, and they used the best of the folk repertoire in language and narrative.

In this volume, moreover, I am interested in humor and the Plains. I believe that the best humor of the Plains was found in the mouths of the common people, as it was expressed in the streets and as it was expressed in the newspapers. Be it folklore or popular culture, I consider it appropriate to our conversation here in these pages.

The *Harpers New Monthly Magazine* and *Harpers Weekly*, eastern journals that are frequently drawn upon to provide insights to 19th-century America, were lamentably obtuse when it came to humor, especially the tall tale. The sections of the papers set aside for jokes and humor contained primarily English jokes or English-style humor from the eastern United States, and, to adapt Lincoln's words, "Each is duller than the other."

With Germanic stolidness they published articles analyzing and explaining American humor, so that all readers would understand that the jokes were intended to be funny:

> The humor of exaggeration is due to the disproportion between the idea and the expression of the idea and they frequently involve a union of incommensurable magnitudes. Of this kind is much American humor, as "The tree was so high that it took two men and a boy to see to the top of it."[9]

In *The Bear Went Over the Mountain* R. B. Downs suggests that I am not alone in my opinion:

> An influential factor in the development of such folklore, too, was a long tradition of oral story-telling, the importance of which was recognized by an English traveler, Andrew Lang, about 75 years ago. "All over the land in America," Lang wrote, "Men are eternally 'swopping stories,' at bars, and in the long, endless journeys by

railway and steamer. How little, comparatively, the English 'swop stories.' The stories thus collected in America are the subsoil of American literary humor, a rich soil in which the plant grows with vigor and puts forth fruit and flowers."[10]

Perhaps the turmoil of the frontier served as the cultivator of that rich soil for here it put forth super-bounteous crops. Our most venerated patriotic figures did their share of lying and joking, a fact seldom enjoyed by readers of 20th-century schoolbooks:

Of a different character were several yarns invented [sic] by Benjamin Franklin to satirize the ignorance of Englishmen about the New World. Writing in 1765, Franklin relates: "The very tails of the American sheep are so laden with wool, that each has a little car or wagon on four little wheels, to support and keep it from trailing on the ground. . . . Cod, like other fish when attacked by their enemies, fly into any waters where they can be safest; whales when they have a mind to eat cod pursue them wherever they fly; and the grand leap of the whale in that chase up Niagara Falls is esteemed by all who have seen it as one of the finest spectacles in nature."[11]

The tall tale is not uniquely American, but even the practitioners acclaim that it attained—no, soared to—new heights here. In the only, truly funny article published in *Harpers Weekly* during the first ten years of its existence, and this in the very first issue, January 3, 1857,[12] a very vivid account of the transplant of the greatest of all tall-talers was recounted:

BARON MUNCHAUSEN IN AMERICA

The Saxon Penates—the cat, the clock, and the tea-kettle—were dozing about the fire-place. The tea-kettle was singing. Formerly that same kettle was called a toddy-kettle, but then it never sang; who ever heard of a toddy-kettle singing? In those days too, it never had the quiet respectable appearance which belongs to it now; it sat jauntily on the blazing coals, it puffed fitfully, and if left to itself a while, would give sudden lurches to either side, just like some of those who sat around it. The Chinese and Father Matthew have changed all that, and raised the kettle to its proper position. Like all parvenus, it is but too conscious of the honor conferred upon it, and sits all evening singing duets with Mrs. Grimalkin, just as if there were nothing to do on earth but to sing and look prim. Mrs. Grimalkin looks very much like the tea-kettle—the tea-kettle looks very much like Mrs. Grimalkin, therefore they are jealous of one another and both do their best to look very stately; both are ordinarily very grave, though both occasionally spit out their ill temper when left too long at their ease—the Gods of Olympus sometimes quarreled, why not these also, Our Fireside Deities!

A sleepy party were the Saxon Penates and myself. Mrs. G., in her comfortable position on the rug, went pur-r-r-r—pur-r-r-r—pur-r-r-r—Mrs. Tea-Kettle went bur-r-r-r—bur-r-r-r—bur-r-r-r—bur-r-r-r—bur-r-r-r—the clock went tick—tick—tick—tick—and I went nid-nod—nodding—nidding, till suddenly the doorbell rang, startling us all from our dozy attitudes. Mrs. G. scratched her left ear with her right paw; Mrs. T. sneezed, turning a big blazing coal that was right under her nose to deep black; the clock struck ten; and I was in the midst of a comfortable yawn, as the door opened and the servant announced,

"The Baron Munchausen!"

I arose to greet my old friend, who advanced with a springy gait and shook my hand cordially. His face glowed with the same good humor as when we had met last in France; his shining, bald forehead had followed the prevailing mania for annexation, and had encroached considerably on the iron-gray locks that now hung scantily about his ears; rosy red were his head, face, and nose—the last, indeed, more like a claret cork in shape and color than anything else, but everything about him spoke of good-nature. His gesture, expression of countenance, and dress, all invited one to sit down by a good fire, and have a talk, or, rather, to hear a talk, for the Baron rarely allows his friends time to edge in a single word.

Monongahela was soon substituted for souchong; the cat fled; the clock ceased ticking; the kettle puffed fiercely, and the fire blazed brightly—such was the influence of the atmosphere the Baron carried about him.

As soon as I could get a chance, I said, "My dear Munchausen, tell me what has happened since we last met, and by what strange accident you have been induced to visit this country?"

The Baron's eyes twinkled with delight as he moved his chair close to mine and commenced the following narration:

"After I had bid you farewell at Cherbourg, I repaired to the arsenal to meet an officer with whom I was to dine that day. Being extremely fatigued by the long walk I had taken and on account of the heat of the day, I crept into one of the big guns lying there in order to repose a little. I was hardly in a comfortable position before I fell asleep. Unfortunately, it was precisely upon that day that they were celebrating the birth of a prince, and at six o'clock they were preparing to fire a salute in honor of the occasion. The guns had been loaded in the morning and as no one could dream that I was there, wrapped in quiet slumbers, I was suddenly launched with terrible velocity straight across the English Channel. By a miracle I fell upon a haystack on a farm near Southampton, where I remained without awakening, as you may readily imagine, considering the force of the shock.

"About three months after this event there was a rise in the price of hay, so that the farmer began selling and putting away from the stack. I was awakened by the noise of the laborers, who were carting away the hay. Still sleepy, and hardly knowing where I was, I wished to fly, and, in doing, so, fell upon the head of the proprietor. I was but slightly injured by the fall, though the unfortunate farmer rested under me dead, I having, in the most innocent way in the world, broken his neck.

"The affair created great excitement in the neighborhood, and all the peasantry were delighted to be rid of the miserly old fellow, who always hoarded his grain in seasons of scarcity.

"I immediately published a full account of this adventure; but imagine my astonishment, Sir, when, after a few days, I received a note from an influential London journal, requesting me to repair at once to the metropolis upon business of importance to myself and the world.

"In four hours I was in London and in fifteen more closeted with the editor of the Lon--- ------."

The Baron drained his glass, coughed, drew his chair close beside mine, arched his eyebrows, and placing his forefinger on his nose, said, "Hist!"

I histed.

"You Americans are a slandered people, and the edi-

tors of the paper referred to wish to have reliable information respecting you. 'Therefore, Baron,' said one of
them, 'knowing your adventuresome spirit, your high
character for veracity, your integrity, and your habits of
correct observation, we wish to send you as our Special
Correspondent to the United States of America. We wish
you to describe what you see as you see it, without tricks
of rhetoric or fine writing. You will repair thither by the
Persia, travel over the country, "peruse the towns,"
observe the manners of the people, and note your
observations.'

"After these instructions I started immediately and
me voici!"

I was about to speak but the Baron immediately
resumed, "Sir, I lead a terrible life. I am growing thin,
Sir; I am compelled to travel under a feigned name, and
all on account of the excitement caused by my last letter,
in which I related my adventures on a railway in Georgia.
Why, Sir, I considered that one of the best things I ever
wrote. Read all my works, and you will find nothing to
compare with it. In England the narration was highly
appreciated. (Ah Sir, there is good taste, education, and
refinement in England!) The letter, too, was published in
France, Germany, Spain, Austria, Russia, and Italy; it will
circulate in India, China, Australia, and wherever men
read books. Recent events, Sir, make the world pant for
information about your country; and we shall no longer
see half a dozen scanty lines of cotton quotations devoted
to the news from a nation of 30,000,000 people. My letters, Sir, are appreciated wherever truth is spoken. But,
would you believe it, there are some here in America who
dare doubt their veracity. The consequence is, my life is
in continual danger."[13]

I tried to reassure the Baron, and begged him to
relate to me one of his adventures. He glanced furtively at
the door, then at the window, then up the chimney, and
finally commenced an account of his trip down the
Mississippi.

"I started from Louisville," said he, "on the splendid
steamer *Great Blower*. Our voyage was quiet, and
unmarked by incident until we had passed Cairo [Illi-
nois], when on one fine morning, we saw a large steamer
close in our wake, which proved to be the *Screamer*, of St.
Louis, bound for New Orleans. It was a fine sight to see

her plow up the water, and bellow from her great steam-pipes, as she rapidly gained on us; but, from the increasing speed of both boats, and the excitement among our two hundred passengers, I soon discovered that we were racing. You may imagine my fear, Sir, at this discovery, and how gladly I would have got ashore, if that had been possible.

"Our rival was now directly opposite us; the boats nearly touched; the captain of the *Screamer* shook his fist three times at the captain of the *Great Blower*; the captain of the *Great Blower* showed his teeth, and then both captains rushed below. Immediately I saw the hands rolling barrels of lard and tar toward the furnaces. A thick, black smoke belched forth in heavy volumes from the chimneys; the steam pipes groaned hoarsely, making the vast forests on either side roar with the echoes; the wheels spun around with inconceivable velocity, driving our sharp prows through the placid water at a rate of thirty miles an hour. The *Screamer* gains a little, but it is only a momentary advantage, for the hands of the *Great Blower*, leaving the heavy logs of wood, are soon bringing down tables, chairs, looking-glasses, and whatever else was light and dry, dipping them into the tar barrels, and thrusting them into the furnaces. The *Great Blower* now shoots ahead a foot or two; but the noise of axes is heard; the *Screamer* men are cutting away their hurricane deck and pitching the white, dry pine into the glowing grates. The pipes are red hot; the safety valves are fastened down, when suddenly---."

The Baron wiped his forehead and groaned.

"Suddenly, Sir, there came a deep, heavy sound, as of a rumbling under the crust of the earth which, quick as a flash, burst into a loud report; and at the same instant (How long that instant!) I saw the hurricane deck where I was standing rise slowly at first (though all in the same second of time), and then shoot with great velocity, carrying myself and fifty others at least five hundred feet into the air. Our flight was so rapid, Sir, that I involuntarily put my hand to my hat to keep it from flying off, in doing which, it came in contact with a Yankee's nose, and, would you believe it, Sir, he drew his revolver, and ejecting a huge lump of tobacco from his mouth, said, 'Darn your eyes, I'll fix your hash when we git down again.'

"As you may imagine, I endeavored to get down first, but, on alighting I found that long-haired, saffron-faced rascal up to his knees in the swamp, with his revolver cocked, and waiting for me. He threw me another revolver with an oath, telling me to say my prayers quick, and fire as soon as he had counted three.

"I was resigning myself quietly to my fate, when—and would you believe it, Sir—a huge piece of the boiler, which had been driven higher than ourselves, came down upon his head, and crushed the varmint into the swamp.[14]

"I thanked Providence for my deliverance, and was glad to get on another steamer that was passing."

"And what became of the other boat?" I asked.

"They were both blown up, Sir, and one of them sank; but the two captains fell down upon the same wreck. A quarrel immediately ensued, each swearing the boat was his. They were both pointing to a shattered plank with the letters ER on it, and gesticulating furiously.

" 'Fool!' says the one, 'Don't you see ER stands for *Great BlowER!*'

" 'Villain!' says the other, gnashing his teeth, 'Can't you spell *S-c-r-e-a-m-E-R!*'

"Out came the bowie knives. Blood flowed. A fearful lunge of his adversary sent the captain of the *Great Blower* reeling overboard, and in a few minutes we were far away from this awful scene, *which is of almost daily occurrence on the Mississippi River!*"

The Baron added that he would send an account of this adventure on the next packet to the Lon---. Here he sneezed (for the fire had gone out), and without allowing me time to ask the name of the journal for which he was correspondent, he shook my hand warmly, with a "Good-night, Good-night, Good-night, Sir!" and bounded out of the room.

In *Shingling the Fog and Other Plains Lies* I spent a good deal of space emphasizing my contention that one of the features of the Plains tall tale that made it so striking, so appropriate for the homesteader and prairie traveler was its painful nearness to the truth of the matter. The incredibility of the pioneer's stories were parodies of the incredibility of his landscape.

And whenever the geography got to be old hat, the

conditions imposed by man himself reached tall-tale proportions. For example, it is a thoroughly documented truth that banks sprang up everywhere, with little or no real capital, issued their own monies, and eventually created a financial havoc on the Plains and prairies. Stories like the following, then, were only preposterous to the degree that the reality was also preposterous:

> A correspondent in Wisconsin says he arrived out there from the East just after the suspension of specie payments, and gold and silver were not to be seen, and were only known as curiosities of a former and almost forgotten period. He had one dime left and when it became known that he had this amount he was waited on by a committee of citizens, who desired to secure it as a specie basis for a new bank they were about to start.[15]

Nothing, it appeared, in this land was what it seemed, or should seem. Many a hopeful migrant bought a fine lot in Capital City, right between the cathedral and the school, only to find upon his arrival that the town consisted of nothing more than rows of wooden stakes in the open prairie. *Harpers Weekly* reported in 1864, "It is stated to be a rule of war in the far Western Territory that 'a town is a place where whisky is sold.' By means of this rule the courts distinguish real towns from those which exist only on paper plans of land speculators."[16]

Athearn paints an even paler image of the frontier "city":

> Sometimes it was not even necessary to mark off streets and avenues. More than one western town appeared on the map just because some individual erected a building and christened it a city. Ekalaka, Montana, is said to have sprung from such a small seed. As the story goes, a trader whose wagons bogged down in the mud unloaded his stock, principally whiskey, and with the remark, "Hell, any place in Montana is a good place for a saloon," erected a cabin. The town was named after the Indian wife of the bar's first customer, a buffalo hunter. There are many counterparts of Ekalaka in the plains West, some of which never got beyond the one-building stage.
>
> From the work of an unnamed English traveler dur-

ing the post-Civil War years: "At a place called 'La Park,' where there was but one wooden shanty, I heard a gentleman ask its proprietor 'if anyone was then talking about building a second house in that city.' "

The Reverend John H. Blegen, who was searching for a town called Broken Bone, in Dakota Territory, must have had much the same puzzled reaction. Wondering if he had missed his destination, he came to a shanty to which a man was then nailing a sign reading "Grocery Store and Saloon." "Where is Broken Bone?" asked Blegen. "You are right in the heart of the city, sir. This is Main Street, but if you go down the hill, you will find the summer resorts among those trees yonder."[17]

Athearn inventories the styles and degrees of deception and artifice, creating the distinct impression that the frontier town and country were nothing more than smoke dreams:

By the ancient American custom of circumventing those laws not popular, legal stipulations were side-stepped or openly violated. . . . By means of a tin cup cowhands "conducted water on the land," thereby living up to the letter of the [Desert Land Act.] It was the same in Wyoming. Irrigation "ditches" were constructed by plowing a furrow; if the alleged waterways went up and downhill without regard to the contour of the land, the Westerners merely shrugged. They had to do the best they could with the laws Congress conjured up.[18]

Was it the laughers who survived or the survivors who laughed? It's hard to know for sure, but that there was a connection cannot for a moment be denied.

1

BEYOND CIVILIZATION

> Living on the Plains is a lot like being hung: the initial shock is unsettling but hang there long enough and sooner or later you get used to it.
>
> Don Messing, Sidney, Nebraska

> In every bar-room lay a copy of the local paper and every copy impressed it upon the inhabitants . . . that they were the best, finest, bravest, richest, and most progressive town of the most progressive nation under heaven. . . .
>
> Rudyard Kipling

> A group of soil conservationists was making a tour through a badly eroded rocky section of the hill country. At one stop, a farmer told the visitors, "My forefathers fought for this here land." Then looking out across his gullied fields, he added wryly, "They wuz the hotheaded type, I guess."
>
> *The Furrow*

Would-be poets have taken occasional tries at dealing with the frontier and its lore. Few such poetasters or their readers have taken their extravagant claims very seriously however. In fact, it is precisely that obvious extravagance that labels the material "lies" and says, "Look at the fix I'm in!" The following poem was published in the *Juniata* [Nebraska] *Herald* on May 8, 1878; the honesty of the poetic account is perhaps suspect because this same newspaper initiated a two-year flying saucer scare in 1897 that spread throughout the Plains states.[1] The poem was addressed to Sol Crawford in Lake County, Indiana.[2]

IT IS TRUE AS IT IS AWFUL

My old friend Sol, you are too wise
To stay in Lake, and hear their lies;
They say Nebraska is a poor and windy state,
You can tell them for me that all is a mistake.

The wind is no harder, so let your mind rest.
Sell out, young man and emigrate west.
The climate, the weather, the soil is good;
We have plenty of coal but very little wood.

This is a country of plenty I will relate,
Buffalo, elk, antelope, other game too numerous to state.
The wheat heads grow here as long as your arm—
You can take the straw to fence your farm.

The grass grows so large, with all the rest,
That the coon climbs the stalk to build his nest;
The corn grows so large it would make your heart throb
To punch the Jack Rabbits out of the cob!

After seeing the country you will never say
That you are sorry you came to Nebraska.
Money here is so plenty, as sure as you live,
One thousand dollars to a poor emigrant they always do give.

Now Sol, consider well what I have said,
Scratch all the Lake County lice out of your head;
Sell all of your cats, your hay, and your corn,
And start for Nebraska and don't be forlorn.

Sol, get out of the mud, the rain, and the storm;
Come to Nebraska, where it is dry, nice, and warm.
Your hair will turn black, you will feel young again;
You can raise a large family without any pain.

Normally, when one hears arguments on two sides of an issue, the natural tendency is to believe that the truth lies—you should excuse the expression—somewhere in the middle. Life on the Plains changed that: soon one comes to believe here that the truth most certainly and almost always lies somewhere in *both* extremes. I have always admired the word "uncompromising" when describing the Plains. There is no accommodation to the average, no adjustment to the center.

Abundant evidence exists to support this contention of mine. A disproportionate percentage of the nation's record weather extremes, for example, are the unenviable possession of the Plains states. Polarity is the watchword of Plains politics, historically as well as contemporarily. I will deal with the weather at greater length later in this essay, but for the moment let me just note that this year I watched 2000 trees wither and die on my farm as we passed six weeks without a drop of rain. I wondered if it would ever rain again. It did—nine inches in two hours.

So, if you wonder whether the next poem, penned by D. N. Srewolf (sic) in the mid 1890s, is a paean in praise of the Plains or a mumbled curse, the answer is "yes."[3]

NEBRASKA

O gently undulating Plain,
With cities springing up amain,
In summer, one vast field of grain,
    And that's Nebraska.

A climate subject to extremes;
For drainage, four big muddy streams;
Its minerals chiefly in "salines,"
    And that's Nebraska.

A native tree seen here and there;
A coyote racing with a hare,
And night shuts down—you know the rest;
    That was Nebraska.

Long trains of ox teams moving west,
Each red skin waiting for his guest,
And night shuts down—you know the rest;
    That was Nebraska.

The birds a-singing in the trees,
Among the flowers the honey bees,
Where fans your cheek the softest breeze,
    And that's Nebraska.

A great expanse of bluest sky,
Feathery cloudlets floating by,
A sun so hot you'll almost fry,
    And that's Nebraska.

Twenty below on the Fahrenheit scale,
The wind northwest, and a perfect gale,
The sky grows dark, our cheeks grow pale,
    And that's Nebraska.

The state where Arbor Day was born,
Where apples grow as well as corn,
And every plant that bears a thorn,
    And that's Nebraska.

Where grows the lovely goldenrod,
In countless billions on the sod,
And every weed that's known to God,
    And that's Nebraska.

A soil so rich, and black, and deep,
No other country need compete;
We plant a grain—a bushel reap,
    And that's Nebraska.

School houses dotting all the land,
Here education's march is grand,
Church spires nowhere thicker stand
    Than in Nebraska.

He who comes with us to sup
May find a sweet or a bitter cup,
Of all things good and bad mixed up,
    Here in Nebraska.

Probably every state in the Union, and certainly every region, has its stories that dramatize the salubrious geography with which it and it alone has been blessed. There are stories of the bodies of departed souls being sent back to Nebraska from California, and when the family opens the casket for one last look at the late lamented, just the brush of the Nebraska air on the corpse's nose, or the reflection of one stray beam of Nebraska sunlight, was enough to revive him sufficiently to help with the hay harvest later that same afternoon.

Lowell Thomas, the noted world traveler, once assembled a collection of tall tales sent to him by his radio audience[4] and several told of dead or dying people being revived merely by a whiff of air from an automobile or bicycle tire that had been inflated with the healthful air of some wonderfully climated state or another.

Coloradoans maintained that the air of that state was so good that it was impossible to get sick—even if one wanted to. A citizen of the state told an English visitor, "I once knew a man who tried to make himself ill in order to get off serving on a jury. He ate nothing but fat pork and drank nothing but lemonade for a week, but he couldn't do it, sir. The air you breathe in Colorado enables you to avoid anything."[5]

The *Nebraska Independent Pen and Plow* on December 9, 1880, indirectly noted the dilemmas arising from living in such a wholesome climate as that found on the Plains:[6]

That's a fact thank the good Lord. Our Oakdale undertakers are getting so gloomy that they have to wheel their drooping jaws and lower lips in wheelbarrows before them. Not long ago a man over 200 years old was accidentally killed, and as there wasn't a copy of the church burial service in the county, the parson sent off the departing soul with choice extracts from the Declaration of Independence.

Nor were the benefits of the Plains climate and soil squandered only on men. A report from 1868 indicates that the crops of the period were equally benefited:[7]

Everybody knows that from twenty to thirty bushels of wheat is the average crop during good seasons in Nebraska. Everybody knows that in the St. Louis market Nebraska wheat brings the highest and fanciest prices. Almost everybody knows also that it is quite a common thing for farmers to raise enough wheat during the first year to pay for their land, pay for plowing it and fencing it.

Upon their wheat crops Nebraska farmers brag. A few of them were bantering each other on the subject recently, when one of them having heard the others first, declared that, in 1867, he raised eighty acres of wheat which stood so thick and heavy on the ground that he was compelled to rent a quarter section of land adjoining it to shock it upon! There wasn't room in the field where the wheat grew. . . .

Which is not to suggest that everyone recognized or appreciated the glories of Plains pioneer life. On occasion a homesteader who imagined greener fields would abandon the Plains and while his friends could never understand such a decision, it is clear from the following editorial published in 1907 in the *Sidney* [Nebraska] *Telegraph* that they could at least sympathize:[8]

Occasionally a good man grows dissatisfied with Nebraska. The milk is too yellow or the honey too sweet and he doesn't like them to flow over his land anyway. So he parts with his farm, sells his livestock and other things too numerous to mention and moves to Oklahoma. There he takes his good Nebraska money and buys a farm which today is and tomorrow is not, because the wind has blown it away. Or he tries Colorado and slushes around in the mud irrigating a strip of bottom so narrow that a cow can't jump into the field because she jumps over it. Then he hears of Texas and goes down to hunt the bag of gold at the rainbow. In the daytime he scratches sandburs out of his flesh and at night centipedes crawl over his face. When his money is all gone he begins to feel like he did the first night he ever stayed away from home. He yearns for good old Nebraska and the yearn sticks in his throat and chokes him until tears come in his eyes. He would give a month's work to see the cows standing at the bars on his old Nebraska farm and hear the horn blow for supper. Memory is a marvelous painter and paints the best things we love best. It pictures to the traveler the corn silking in the field he once owned, and the wheat yellowing for the harvest, for the land, the clover stretching away in a carpet of red and green, richer than the rugs of Persians. It shows him the elms as they whispered to his children at play beneath them, points to the roses in the corner of the old rail fence, and in infinite detail paints a thousand things that touch the heart and prove its whimsical power. Happy is the man who wakes from sleep to find that he has wandered from Nebraska only in his dreams.

That kind of boasting is predictable. On the other hand, imagine the appeal that the following story from the September 24, 1925, issue of the *Frontier* (O'Neill, Nebraska) must have had when it hit the newspaper desks of the Degenerate East![9]

Investigation of several cases of intoxication among the children attending the annual picnic of the Sunday school of Lost Pond Union Church, six miles below Beaver Flats, last week, has led to the exonerations of the ranchman on whose lands the picnic was held and the unearthing of evidence of perhaps a tragedy happening years before the settling of Calamus Valley.

Considerable indignation was aroused during the picnic when a number of the elder boys who had gone over from the picnic grounds to an old abandoned orchard a quarter of a mile away returned displaying alarming evidences of inebriation and breaths of a decidedly Kentucky aroma. Search of the old orchard disclosed no apparent source of supply, and the boys were brought before Judge Kirwin in the Beaver Flats Juvenile Court next day in an effort to ascertain the identity of their bootlegger. All, however, indignantly denied that they had partaken of intoxicants and insisted that they had done nothing but eat a few apples.

As only a few of the boys who had visited the orchard had shown signs of intoxication, the Court at first refused to believe them. Further questioning, however, elicited that only those who had eaten from a tree on the extreme south side of the orchard, and on the edge of what the early settlers said had been a former channel of the Calamus River, were affected.

The Court to assure himself that the youths were not lying, ordered an adjournment, and with the court attaches and a number of the leading citizens of the Flats visited the orchard and sampled the fruit of the tree from which the boys declared they had partaken. The apples proved to be of delicious and peculiar flavor and the eating of several of them imparted a decided feeling of warmth and exhilaration.

Judge Kirwin immediately ordered the Sheriff to destroy the tree, both trunk and roots. While digging out the latter the workmen, in following up a lone one, came across an old and well preserved barrel six feet below the surface, into which tentacles of the root had forced an entrance around the bung. The head of the cask at once was knocked in and it was found to still contain several gallons of a thick and oily liquid which evidently once had been whiskey. The liquid was taken in possession of by the officials and turned over to the Beaver Flats Hospital. The barrel is supposed to have been a part of the cargo of a steamboat said to have sunk in the river at about this point years ago when river traffic was at its height.

Do not be embarrassed if you have not previously heard of the Calamus River; it is a stream in the northwestern quarter of Nebraska which can be traveled by canoe—during wet springs.

And if stories like this could appear as plain truth in the local rag—[10]

Mr. Wilson of Beatrice [Nebraska] runs a water cart, which is a large tank balanced upon two wheels, and drawn by one horse. As he was coming up the street a few days ago the wheels of his cart struck a street crossing and sent the water with a rush to the back end of the tank, broke the belly band, and lifted the horse high in the air, where he hung from the shafts of the cart. It took two or three men to balance down the shafts and put the horse on the ground.

then who would question one like this in the same newspaper:[11]

The big corn story liar is abroad in the land. One of the South Platte country exchanges gets off the following: "The little son of Mr. B-- living west of town got a ladder the other day and stood it up against a cornstalk. He then took a saw and climbed up about twenty feet to the first ear, he proceeded to straddle the ear and saw it off, but unfortunately he sawed between himself and the stalk and he was thrown to the ground, breaking his arm." That's the story. Now then, somebody hold our coat! We didn't intend mentioning the fact that has come to our knowledge, but when a South Platte prevaricator attempts to down this section of the corn question, we will read him facts. Last Saturday in conversation with Ed Jenkins the reporter learned that an illicit distillery was in operation in one of the ravines near his residence and the government was therefore being defrauded out of a large amount of revenue. It appears that a man arrived in that neighborhood, and one night, with the aid of a gang of laborers, dynamite, crowbars, etc., succeeded in prying off a kernel of corn from a big prize ear in Ed's field. It was then loaded onto a stoneboat and hauled into the ravine. The man then bored into the kernel of corn with a two-inch auger, put in a faucet, and now has an unlimited supply of pure corn juice on tap.

Corn was probably the most important crop next to kids and mortgages on the Plains (and third to those also in yield) so it is not surprising that there is an abundance of tall tales about it. If the next two selections[12] prove anything at all, they underline emphatically, in my opinion, the hopeless tactical position of the man who tells the first story.

A Missourian informed a traveler who inquired about his corn that each stalk had nine ears on it and was fifteen feet high.

"That's nothing to our corn," replied the traveler. "Up in Illinois, where I came from, we always had nine ears to each stalk, and a peck of shelled corn hanging on each tassel, but we could never raise any field beans with it."

"Why?"

"Because the corn grew so fast that it always pulled the beans up."

* * *

Early in the forenoon Dr. Binninger, Tom Fenton, Jim Hart, the retired miner, and Frazer, the Canadian, came up and began inspecting the crops.

"Oh, this is very well; very well, indeed, for Jersey," said Dr. Binninger, at last, as they sat on the fence by the cornfield, after their labors, smoking; "But nothing to what I have seen. In Gastley County, Missouri, I once saw the corn growing to such an unprecedented height, and the stalks so exceptionally vigorous, that nearly every farmer stacked up, for winter firewood, great heaps of cornstalks, cut up into cord-wood length by power saws run by the threshing engines. One man, Barney Gregory, took advantage of the season to win a fortune by preparing cornstalks for use as telegraph poles. . . ."

"What is one man's meat is another man's poison," said Fenton. "Fine growing weather, similar to that which made Gregory's fortune in Missouri, has come near ruining those of the Western Nebraska farmers who raised pumpkins. Just as, by all ordinary rules, the crop should have been ready to house, a mysterious rot began to destroy the great green globes glowing to yellow in the sun. An examination by the chemists of the State Agricultural College showed that the trouble was due to the too rapid growth of the vines, which dragged the pumpkins about after them, all over the fields until the pumpkins' lower cuticle, being worn out by the abrasion, they succumbed easily to rot in the bruised portion. Should another such year come, the farmers will avoid a like catastrophe by providing each pumpkin with a straw-lined nest or a little truck with casters.

"A good illustration of nature's bounty happened some time ago in Doniphan County, Kansas," continued Fenton. "A seven-year-old daughter of James Steele was sent, in the middle of the forenoon, to carry a jug of switchel[13] to the men, who were at work near the middle of one of those vast Kansas cornfields. The corn was about up to little Annie's shoulders as she started, but as she went along it rose and rose before her eyes, shooting out of the soil under the magic influence of the sun and the abundant moisture. Almost crazed with fear, she hastened on, but before she could reach the men, the stalks were waving above her head. The men were threatened in a like manner, but by mounting a little fellow on a big man's shoulders, to act as a lookout, they managed to get out, when they promptly borrowed a dog, to follow little Annie's trail. It was not until late in the afternoon, that they reached her, where she lay, having cried herself to sleep with the tear-stains streaking her plump cheeks."

"The soil of some of the Southern California counties is so rich as to become an actual detriment to the farmer," observed Eckels. "In San Bernadino County, a farmer, named Jones, has been forced entirely to abandon the culture of corn, because the stalks, under the influence of the genial sun, mild air, and mellow soil, shoot up into the air so fast that they draw their roots after them; when, of course, the plant dies as a rule. Cases have been known, however, where cornstalks thus uprooted, and lifted into the air, have survived for some time upon the climate alone."

"Why," said Dr. Binninger, "we used to have the same trouble in Kentucky, but it was solved long ago by burying a heavy stone under each cornstalk and wiring the stalk down to it. I have known the price of stone to treble in one season in consequence of the purely agricultural demand."

Which presumably left the whole session at a stand-off.

It is well known that it is not possible to introduce such radical departures into an ecology without profoundly influencing other conditions of that ecology, because all things are inextricably interrelated. So it was too on the Plains frontier. The new crops instituted changes in the pioneers' environment right down to the kinds of sounds he could expect to hear at night:[14]

By placing your ear to the ground a deep rumbling noise can be distinctly heard. It comes from the country and is caused by the pumpkins and squash being dragged over the ground by the rapid growth of the vines, and the potatoes jostling each other in their good-natured strife to win the red ribbon at the Dodge County fair this fall. That whirring musical sound, heard by day and night, is caused by the growing of the corn.

There *were* bad years. A farmer in Utica, Nebraska, told me in March of 1975 that he had had such a bad corn crop the year before that he had just put a hog in the wagon and tossed the ears of corn directly into the wagon to it. At noon he changed hogs.

In fact, most of the years were bad years—still are—and the power of that fact is emphasized precisely by the absurdity of the exaggeration. The brags of the farmers were no more believed than were those of the chambers of commerce. Indeed, it was precisely during the worst years that the stories were told of corn crops so big that loggers and electrical company linemen were hired to harvest it or grass so lush that farmers would go out into the field and drive on top of the grass and plow until they got down to the dirt.[15] I have however heard some recent stories that are reflections, slightly magnified, of realities. A few years ago soya beans were selling at an all-time high price and it was reported that a farmer near Arlington, Nebraska, tried to pay for a cup of coffee in the local restaurant with two soya beans; the cashier however would not accept the beans because he didn't have that much change on hand.

At the current date, the early 1980's, land prices on the Plains are unbelievably high, which also results in some strange occurrences. The David City *Banner-Press* reported in November, 1971, that an area farmer didn't show up at a VFW affair one evening and a friend called to tell him that he had better get to town in a hurry. The farmer ignored the advice and stayed in bed. Some of his friends went to the farm in an ambulance and took him into town on a stretcher. The victim, it was reported, didn't mind the whole deal so much except that his neighbors thought he'd had a heart attack and were calling to rent his land.[16]

Mrs. F. W. Stevens of Orleans, Nebraska, was moved to verse in 1918 to describe the phenomenal conditions she saw all around her:[17]

NEBRASKA

They talk about Nebraska storms
And its various kinds of weather,
But I prefer its fertile soil
And the crops we have to gather.

'Twas in the early days, forsooth,
I went out to my garden.
I took my infant son along
His little limbs to harden.

I placed him in a furrow rich,
A twelve-foot ladder found
And, mounting, gathered roasting ears
While he played on the ground.

I heard a pig a-squealing loud
Out in a field quite near.
I looked across from my high perch;
He was racing like a deer.

A pumpkin vine was chasing him
And gaining on him fast;
It caught him, passed him, ran ahead—
It truly made me laugh.

It reached the fence, it ran on through,
A pumpkin forming there;
The pig still running for the fence,
The vine had beat him there.

I then climbed down to get my son
And go home to get dinner.
He stood there six feet four, 'tis true,
The fertile soil, the winner.

So prate about Nebraska storms
And its various kinds of weather,
But I will take its fertile soil
And the crops we have to gather.

Until the Plainsmen became used to the new conditions, they were not without their serious dangers:[18]

. . . A young man living near Hooper, Nebraska, was once saved a nasty accident by the exuberance of Nebraska crop growth. It was in November, 1895, and he had gone up alongside a cornstalk, using a fifteen-foot stepladder, and was chopping off an ear of corn with a hatchet. He slipped from the ladder and hurtled downward, but very luckily fell on a 160-pound pumpkin and was eased to the ground.

The greatest danger was the damage that might come to one's reputation upon telling some cynic from the East about the wonders of the Great American Desert. Records suggest that the talkative homesteader had to defend his honor against doubters more often than he had to defend his home against Indians:[19]

"Do you call them large turnips?"
"Why yes, they are considerable large."
"They may be for turnips but they are nothing to an onion I saw the other day."
"And how large was the onion?"
"Oh, a monster, it weighed forty pounds."

"Forty pounds?"

"Yes, we took off the layers, and the sixteenth layer went around a demijohn that held four gallon."

"What a whopper!"

"You don't mean to say I tell a falsehood?"

"Oh no! What a whopper of an onion, I mean."

Perhaps the most impressive factor of the monstrous produce that grew on the frontier was the resourcefulness of the pioneers in dealing with it. Time and again the modern mind is astonished by the fine degree of ingenuity demanded and granted on the frontier:[20]

There was . . . the story of how Moses Stocking went into sheep. He had an acre of bottom land broke . . . but because it was late he couldn't sow anything except turnips. The seed was bad and only five plants came up, one in each corner and one in the middle. But they grew pretty well. The corner ones were squashed and flattened, of course, being so close together, and too puny for any real use—although they hauled one of them to the top of a hill somewhere along the Platte, and when it was hollowed out and the wind dried it, it was used for a military academy and did very well for years to house the boys.

Another turnip that grew in a corner was used for the railroad depot at Omaha, since there would be only temporary use for a depot there. The other two corner turnips were wasted, as I recall; but the one in the center was worth saving and from it grew the Stocking fortune. After walking around it once and coming back footsore and with cockleburs in his beard, Old Moses took the train for Chicago and bought up all the sheep at the stock-market and for the next month there was a stream "as wide as the Missouri" of sheep coming across Iowa to the Stocking place. They started eating at the turnip where Moses blasted a hole, and they lived there all winter, fat and snug, not having to go into the blizzard cold at all but just eating out the pulp; and the shell made a shelter for the sheep—enough of them to keep Jay Cooke[21] afloat for a whole year after he really was broke, only the public didn't know it.

A similar solution from another authority:[22]

We are told there is a man down at Ashland

[Nebraska] who, when he wants to set the posts for a
fence, plants parsnip seed a year before, and when he gets
ready to build the fence he pulls up the parsnips and
drops the posts into the holes. Says he has one growing
now that he intends to pull and then wall up the hole for
a cistern.

The disinherited, often illiterate and poor homesteaders
found the new soil to their liking. The results were frequently interesting:[23]

An enthusiastic exchange says that Nebraska takes
the pot when you come to talk about fertile soil. A
farmer planted a small house, 10 x 12, on his quarter section, and the next year it had grown into a large and com-
modious farm house with green blinds and veranda
attachment. His pump had grown into a windmill, and
instead of one cow had a whole herd. His land had run
over its boundary, and covered three quarters of a section. He had grown from a slim, dyspeptic person to an
individual of over 200 pounds, and his pocket book has
grown so heavy he has had to invest in government
bonds.

And the results were at other times incredible![24]

. . . [There were] two daughters of a farmer living in
the Big Sandy Valley. The oldest daughter, thirteen,
weighed 470 pounds and measured six feet around the
waist. The other girl, seven years old, weighed 175
pounds and had a mid span of four and a half feet. . . .
These girls could have three or four lovers hugging them
at the same time and none of them would know that the
others were around. Either the farmer was extravagant or
he simply could not count. He surely had material
enough for more than two daughters.

The modern reader gains the impression that Plains
pioneer newspapers were filled with the most preposterous
announcements:[25]

Editor Rodman . . . of the *Wausa* [Nebraska] *Times*
says that the bridge builders up there are using the huge
corn stalks for pilings.

John Ashley claims the ears of corn are so high up
on the stalks in his field out on the Blackbird that he will
have to shoot them off.

But notice that wherever the editors were not absolutely sure of the truth of the accounts they prefaced the assertions with words like "says" or "claims." It is for this reason that it seems entirely logical to assume that the articles that do not contain such hedging terms and *caveats* are Truth.[26]

> Last week a farmer under the irrigation ditch near Beverly planted some cucumber seed and before he got through planting the vines came up and entwined around his legs until he couldn't walk. He grabbed a corn knife, but before he could cut the vines loose, they ran up his back and held his arms as in a vise. Fortunately for the poor man, his lung power was good and he yelled like an Indian. Some boys who were attracted by his screams, lassoed him and dragged him from the patch. When he was restored to consciousness all his pockets were found to be full of ripe cucumbers.

In a good many cases the newspaper editor would make it quite clear that he himself doubted the story but would pass it along anyway so that those in possession of supporting facts or evidence could come forward:[27]

> This must have happened a good many years after the Sconebans had come to what is now Nebraska. There were several small settlements scattered around, and two larger towns, one of which was Chemburg, where the inventive McCandos hung out and where the genius of this clan had caused some factories to be erected. The other, and largest town, was Parasite, seat of the Sconeban government. The capital city had been deliberately built some distance away from the rest of the commonwealth, for the good of the people, Hub says.
>
> For some time the citizens of Chemburg had been enjoying the benefits of a McCando invention for storing up the cold of winter for use in the summer. Their dwellings and other buildings were always comfortable, even on the hottest days. And Hub says no one ever complained that the contrast between inside and outside was too great. Governor McErc, on a visit to Chemburg, had seen how successful the cold scheme was and expressed a wish that Parasite, down nearer the Great Mirage (years later called the Platte), might be supplied with coolness in summer. Since Chemburg already had the equipment, the

current McCando agreed to pipe cold from that town to Parasite. Since no iron or other ores had yet been discovered, McCando proposed to use corn stalks for pipes, and in order to grow them large enough to answer the purpose he was going to prepare the seed with a solution of the newly developed nito-vito seed wash. This had been tried out on oats and some other things, but not on corn.

When corn planting time drew near, the chemists made up the solution and put the seed corn in it. McCando and his assistants were also greatly engrossed at this time with their work in perfecting self-milkers for the dairy herd of Scobu cows which had been built up from the first crosses between the native buffalo and Highland cattle the original Sconebans had brought from the old country. The machine was simple, being a system of suction cups and tubes operated by the motion of the cows' jaws as they chewed their cuds. The trouble was in getting the cows to chew their cuds always at milking time. Three of the herd were fairly well trained to this when one evening a green hand fed them some of the new humsorg. This made the cows belch and the action of the self-milkers was reversed. The cows thought they were calves again and butted things around in rare shape. McCando was so agitated by this that he forgot about the seed corn and let it stay too long in the nito-vito wash.

The corn was planted, about 1600 acres of it, and although it did not come up with such alarming rapidity as had the first nito-vito oats, yet it made such growth that it could not be worked. The field was some little distance from Chemburg and, seeing it could not be cultivated, the Chemburgers paid no attention to it during the summer. They figured it would be ready for harvest about the first of September, that is, if it grew and matured at the rate it had started out. Along toward the last of July some little boys got lost one day. A search was begun and they were finally tracked to the cornfield, or rather, the corn forest, for that was what it had become. The seed had been planted eight feet apart and now the trunks of the corn trees almost touched. The boys were found, but a new problem had presented itself. Even to the doughty Sconebans with their double-bitted axes the task of felling the corn trees seemed enormous.

McCando was equal to the emergency. There were thousands of beaver in the streams around Chemburg. Several dozen were caught and fetched to the corn forest. The beaver seemed interested and investigated the corn trees thoroughly but did not set to work felling any of them. Something was lacking, and McCando soon figured out that the lack was water. A beaver would not fell a tree unless there was water nearby. This was a predicament. But a McCando was never stumped, not even by a forest of corn trees. Rushing to the glass works, he got the mechanics there to cut some curly-cues and wavy lines through these rollers. When the molten glass was run through them the result was an effect of rippling in the finished glass. This glass was made up into spectacles and a pair fitted to each beaver that was to work in the corn forest.

This was all that was needed. The beavers, seeing shining water everywhere, felled trees like mad. All the adult males of the vicinity had to work keeping the felled trees out of the way of the working animals, but this was done with the aid of the powerful Scobu oxen. The ears were sawed off from the trunks with the compressed air saw, with a blade of flint, quartered with the same implement and each quarter loaded onto a cart pulled by six head of oxen. Thus the crop was harvested. The stalks were trimmed and cored, by the compressed air corer, and stacked away to season. By another summer the cold line was laid to Parasite and that city got the cooling effects of McCando ingenuity. Even the vehemently boiling atmosphere of the state house was made more temperate.

That's the way it nearly always is with old Hub. He starts out to tell about one thing and when he finally winds up he's told two or three more things.

Whenever necessary an editor would outright debunk a tale he felt was not in the best interests of honesty. In the *Crete Daily Globe* on September 3, 1884, for example, the editor scoffed at Easterners who reportedly believed that Nebraska soil was so rich that one need only stick shingle nails into the ground at night to harvest crowbars in the morning, or for that matter stick a crowbar in the ground and the next morning harvest several pounds of shingling nails.[28]

It was natural enough that eventually such stories would develop in the East about the West. The irony was the people who had never seen the Plains made up wonders like that immediately above but were just as likely to scoff at reliable reports like this below, printed on April 9, 1897, in the *Red Cloud Chief*:[29]

A Webster County [Nebraska] farmer wrote to his friend in the east trying to give him some idea of the soil out here. He said they had to mow the grass of the sod floor to find the baby. One family had twin babies with only one cradle and the kid that had to sleep on the floor grew twice as fast as the other one. Where the soil was the richest a man dare not stand on one foot any length of time lest one leg become longer than the other and bother him in walking.

Quite seriously, these stories do show us the attitudes of wonder with which the conditions of the Plains were met by the immigrants. Of course the tellers and their audience were laughing inside—never outwardly—when they passed on such whoppers, but the fact remains that what they found when they came to the Great American Desert was to them no less preposterous than the tall tales they now inflicted on greenhorns, dudes, New Yorkers, and other gullibles of that ilk.

Walter Webb in his classic *The Great Plains*[30] counted this unique combination of conditions as a major factor in the formation of the Plains mentality and history—and, I submit, of its folklore. Webb wrote,

If the Great Plains forced man to make radical changes, sweeping innovations in his way of living, the cause lies almost wholly in the physical aspects of the land. A study of these physical aspects—land formation, rainfall, vegetation, and animal life—not only illuminates the later historical development, but in large measure serves to explain it.

The five weather phenomena—hot winds and chinooks, northers, blizzards, and hailstorms—are all localized in the Great Plains country. Four of the five bring distress and economic ruin to man and beast and crop; yearly they take their toll, amounting in the aggregate to millions of dollars; they are a significant part of the unusual conditions which civilization had to meet and overcome in the Great Plains.

And yet Webb was far too conservative in his assessment and inventory of the influential climatic and geographic conditions that strained the spirit. The settlers of the Plains had rarely before in their experience encountered tornados, such low temperatures (North Dakota: -60°, South Dakota: -58°, Nebraska -47°, Kansas: -40°), extremely high temperatures (North Dakota: 121°; South Dakota: 120°; Nebraska: 118°; Kansas: 121°), extremely rapid changes (rises of 83° in twelve hours and 49° in two minutes; falls of 84° in twelve hours and 47° in fifteen minutes), modest rainfall or flashfloods.[31] Here they also encountered for the first time the rattlesnake, prairie dog, buffalo, elk, and antelope. Here they caught their first sight of the snow-capped Rocky Mountains that dwarfed the mountains of their previous experience. Accustomed to fighting trees as the worst weed—chopping out saplings, burning out stumps, grubbing up roots—here they found trees rarer even than dollar bills, and *they* were few and far between.[32] Whereas their homelands had been three-fourths rock that had to be tossed from the plow moldboard every three steps, here there were not enough stones in a thousand acres to build a chimney. German farmers who had tilled a fifteen-acre spread and walked to and from their fields from a cozy home in a village now had at least 160 acres to till and they had to live on it, in devastating isolation.

The clarity of the smoke-free air added to that isolation, to the distances seen. Even today that clarity can confuse the visitor.[33]

> On a vivid sunshiny or soft hazy day this small belt of desert further prepared the emigrants for wonders to come by the seeming magic of deceptive distances and mirage. To Mrs. Ferris [a diarist on the Oregon Trail in Nebraska], "A half dozen crows will look like men . . . , a battered stove-pipe becomes a skulking Pawnee." To McBride a dozen men walking ahead looked "like giants 14 or 15 feet high," while "horses look double their natural life."

Another example of the same phenomenon, mentioned so often in early accounts and diaries:[34]

A correspondent in Georgetown, Colorado, vouches for the truthfulness of the following: It is well known that in high altitudes, owing to the rarified air, objects are visible at a great distance; and from the city of Denver, the Rocky Mountains, although some sixteen miles distant, seem but a very short way off. An English gentleman, a tourist, came in on the Kansas Pacific train one morning, fresh from the old country, stopped at the Inter-Ocean Hotel in Denver and soon made the acquaintance of two of the "old citizens." The Britisher was captivated with the appearance of the mountains and suggested to the two "old citizens" that, as the mountain range was such a very short distance from the city, they should all take a walk to it and return in time for dinner. The two "old citizens" saw a chance for some fun, and immediately consented. The trio started west, and walked toward the mountains for some two hours and a half and the mountains were as far away as ever. The Englishman was a good walker and kept a little in advance of his friends. Finally they saw him deliberately sit down, as he came to a small irrigating ditch, perhaps two feet wide, and began taking off his boots and stockings. When they came up to where he was sitting they asked him, in some surprise, what he was doing that for. The Englishman said he was was going to wade the stream. Both the "old citizens" looking at him in astonishment asked him why he didn't step across it. "Step across it!" replied the Britisher, "Step across it! Not I! What do I know about distances in your blarsted country!"

Elsewhere the flatness of the countryside magnified the distances even more. A friend[35] told me that where he comes from, it's so flat that if you stand on a brick you can see ten miles.

There were few geographic phenomena that had the decency to behave like their counterparts in other areas of the world. People had come to think that a river would at least be a river, anywhere in the world, but such was not the case on the Plains. The Missouri River, so solidly clogged with Plains topsoil that natives measure it by the acre rather than the gallon, amazed travelers like Mark

Twain during their visits to the Plains, but what is remarkable about the following account is that unlike Twain's description the truth is not stretched in the least:[36]

"Never took a trip up the Missouri River?" asked a traveling man of two English tourists who were westward bound on a Northern Pacific train.

"Nevah, you know," responded one of the foreign travelers. "This is our first journey, you know, in this blasted country."

"Well, there are some remarkable things about that river," continued the traveling man, "that will be worth your while to visit. Now, to begin with, you know that it is very swift, so swift, in fact, that if a person falls in and drowns, his body is seldom ever recovered. The current is so swift that it carries the lifeless remains downstream for miles and the only hope for recovering them is that the floater will come to the top and will be seen and recovered at some town miles and miles below the place of the accident."

"Most remarkable," chimed in the two foreigners.

"But that is not what I started to tell you," said the traveling man. "I intended to tell you of the crooked course of that stream. It is the longest river in the world if measured by its crooks and turns, but is only respectable in length if measured in a straight line from its source to its mouth.

"Its bends are something wonderful and, of course, make a journey up and down on a steamboat something to be dreaded. As a sample of the bends, I remember one not far above Omaha that is seventy-five miles around and only three quarters of a mile through. In fact, you can see the river across the neck of land. Passengers very often get off and spend a day in hunting and walking across, catch the boat as she comes around the bend. You should come down the Missouri and see some of its beauties."

"We'll make a note of that," remarked one of the interested auditors, "and see it on our way back, don't you know."

A Missouri River pilot had to be a fortuneteller to be successful. It was not enough to know the river, because in the weeks between trips the River could change enough to be a totally different course, miles from where it had been on the previous trip. The River changed beds so often that its nickname was, understandably, The Old Harlot. Twain was a river pilot himself and when he wrote or spoke of the Missouri or Mississippi it was with the inevitable combination of love and distrust that grew within those who knew the river:[37]

> The Mississippi between Cairo and New Orleans was twelve hundred and fifteen miles long one hundred and seventy-six years ago. It was eleven hundred and eighty after the cut-off of 1722. It was one thousand and forty after the American Bend cut-off. It has lost sixty-seven miles since. Consequently, its length is only nine hundred and seventy-three miles at present.
>
> Now, if I wanted to be one of those ponderous scientific people, and "let on" to prove what had occurred in the remote past by what had occurred in a given time in the recent past, or what will occur in the far future by what has occurred in late years, what an opportunity is here! Geology never had such a chance, nor such exact data to argue from! Nor "development of species," either! Glacial epochs are great things, but they are vague—vague. Please observe:
>
> In the space of one hundred and seventy-six years the Lower Mississippi has shortened itself two hundred and forty-two miles. That is an average of a trifle over one mile and a third per year. Therefore, any calm person, who is not blind or idiotic, can see that in the Old Oölitic Silurian Period, just a million years ago next November, the Lower Mississippi River was upward of one million three hundred thousand miles long, and stuck out over the Gulf of Mexico like a fishing-rod. And by the same token any person can see that seven hundred and forty-two years from now the Lower Mississippi will be only a mile and three-quarters long, and Cairo and New Orleans will have joined their streets together, and be plodding comfortably along under a single mayor and a mutual board of aldermen. There is something fascinating about science. One gets such wholesale returns of conjecture out of such a trifling investment of fact.

Now, to be sure, that essay is directed at the Mississippi, but however much smaller the Missouri might be in size, it is in no way lesser in reputation. Athearn writes that old-timers were heard to say that the Missouri was the last of the rivers created by God and was made with all the slops left over from the other rivers.[38] In fact, the murky and muddy nature of this river was even more often commented on than was its sinuosity:[39]

The dust blows out of the Missouri River. It is the only river in the world where the dust blows in great columns out of the river bed. The catfish come up to the surface to sneeze. From the great wide-stretching sandbars on the Kansas shore great columns of dust and sand, about two thousand feet high, come whirling and sweeping across the river and hide the town, and sweep through the train and make everything so dry and gritty that a man can light a match on the roof of his mouth. The Missouri River is composed of six parts of sand and mud and four parts of water. When the wind blows very hard it dries the surface of the river and blows it away in clouds of dust. It is just dreadful. The natural color of the river is seal-brown, but when it rains for two or three days at a time, and gets the river pretty wet, it changes to a heavy iron-gray. A long rain will make the river so thin it can easily be poured from one vessel into another, like a cocktail. When it is ordinarily dry, however, it has to be stirred with a stick before you can pour it out of anything. It has a current of about twenty-nine miles an hour, and perhaps the largest acreage to the square inch that was ever planted. Steamboats run down the Missouri River. So do newspaper correspondents. But if the river is not fair to look upon, there is some of the grandest country on either side of it the sun has ever shone upon. How such a river came to run through such a paradise is more than I can understand.

All of this amazement about the Missouri would have simply been meat for conversation were it not for the fact that the river was the major medium for transportation during the frontier and settlement years. The river steamer was a phenomenon developed specifically to deal with the peculiarities of Plains-prairie rivers just as Plains frontier humor was developed specifically to deal with the general demands of the geography. The steamers drew only a few feet of water and were outfitted with equipment to walk them, quite literally, over sandbars. They were flimsy and cheap, a reflection of the reality that the life of a steamship on the Missouri was certain to be short. The captains, their taste for drink, their language, their readiness to race, and their ingenuity were notorious:[40]

> Crossing a sandbar was a moment of great tension for both passengers and crew. The drama of the situation is illustrated by a story told of a captain whose vessel was at the critical point, halfway over a bar, with engines straining to the breaking point, when a woodchopper came down the bank and scooped up a bucketful of the river. Above the pounding of engines and the groaning of the overloaded equipment, the captain's voice was heard as he roared, "Hey, you put that back!"

River captains were necessarily tough, confident men. The incredible demands of the ships, the rivers, the passengers, the cargo, and the crew provided ample reason for their legendary capacity for whiskey:[41]

> The newspaper item was right which records the accident of the sloop wreck on the North River in September last, in these few but graphic words: While the storm was at its height the vessel keeled to the larboard and the captain and another cask of whiskey rolled overboard.

That item suggests that captains in general were prone to the bottle, and the next suggests that the river captains were representative:[42]

> The upper Missouri River steamboats . . . would run on a light dew an' certainly they used to get by where there was mighty little water. X. Beidler an' his friend, Major Reed, are traveling by boat to Fort Benton. One night they drink more than they should. X. is awakened in the morning by the cries of Reed. On entering his stateroom, X. finds Reed begging for water, as he's dying of thirst.
>
> X. steps to the bedside, and takin' his friend's hand, says, "I'm sorry, friend, I can't do anything for you. That damned pilot got drunk, too, last night and we're eight miles up a dry coulee!"

But whatever the problems that should confront the

captain, the passengers could be counted on to contribute their own energies toward the most practical solution:[43]

> The colonel was an addition to any company, especially the special one who were going from Wheeling to St. Louis at that special time. Somebody who had his well-being at heart said to the old man, "Colonel, ain't you rather afraid to drink so much whiskey?"
>
> "Gentlemen," said the colonel, "it isn't at all my style. I never drink whiskey at home, and I am only doing it now out of consideration for the Captain."
>
> "For the Captain?" queried half a dozen voices.
>
> "Yes, gentlemen, for the Captain. The Captain has stated to me that the water in the river is very low— scurce indeed, very. Do you think gentlemen, that I would under the circumstances use any of the precious fluid, perhaps preventing the boat from getting down the river? I understand my duty to the Captain too well."

The crew too developed special and dedicated loyalties to the commanders of the brave ships that coursed the western rivers:[44]

> We are indebted to a Cincinnati correspondent for this anecdote of Capt. Birch, who is one of the most popular Western steamboat men, a general favorite with the traveling public, and who can both practice and appreciate a good joke. "Passing near the pantry of his boat, he heard one of the cabin-boys indulging quite freely in an inadversion on the officers and crew. Captain Birch turned a very severe countenance upon him and said, 'Young man, hereafter when you have anything to say about anyone on the boat, please except the Captain!"
>
> "A few days later, the Captain happening to be on the deck, the same cabin-boy carried past him a dish prepared for the table, when a pet hog, running between the boy's extremities, completely upset him, effectually disbursing the prepared food. Picking himself up with a most rueful countenance, the boy commenced berating the hog. 'You are the most miserablest hog I ever seen,' when catching a view of the 'Old Man' and remembering his injunction he added 'except the Captain.'
>
> "That boy has had a secure berth on Captain Birch's boats ever since."

Twain had a fine sense of humor, obviously, and many

of the stories of the period suggest that a sense of humor was an essential element of the successful steamboat captain, and it had to extend so far as to enable him to laugh even when the joke was on himself:[45]

> Captain Buckner was stopping for wood on his way down the Mississippi. He thought the pile was too green and he said to the owner, "How long has your wood been cut?" "About four feet," gravely replied the man of wood, and the Captain owed him one.

Life on the river was unusual. The frontier attracted all manner of people and that diversity was reflected on the passenger lists of the steamers. Never was democratic free expression more apparent:[46]

> At one end of the long saloon [on the steamboat] a clergyman was preaching to a small crowd gathered around him; in the middle gambling was in busy progress; and at the one extremity of the saloon there was music and dancing.

The watchword for river travel was adaptability:[47]

> Mr. Jones met Mr. Smith as he was going on board a steamer . . . and asked, "Which way, Smith, up or down?" "That depends upon circumstances," remarked the latter, "If I get a berth over the boiler, I shall probably go up, if in the cabin, down." We have not heard from him since.

Then as now every effort was made to cram the vessel with every possible passenger, every possible piece of cargo. The profit margin was not immense, especially with boats going down (or up, as the case might have been) so frequently. This situation meant that accommodations were rarely luxurious and were more often than not pragmatic:[48]

> One of the most amusing incidents of the late excursion to Rock Island is thus related by *The Utica Telegraph.* A gentleman in the washroom said to the Captain of the boat, "Can't you give me a clean towel, Captain?" "No," said the Captain, "more than fifty persons have used that towel there and you are the first one that's said a word against it!"

> This reminds us of the easy-going chap, who, upon a crowded Western steamer, took up a toothbrush, and

deliberately commenced "scrubbing his grinders." The owner of the instrument, in great indignation, demanded what the individual meant by thus appropriating his private property. "Private!" said the spooney, putting down the ivory and bristles—"*Private!* Why, stranger, I thought this 'ere tooth-cleaner belonged to the boat!"

River steamers were usually so loaded down with cargo, passengers and drink that there was also little attention given to food and its preparation. There is no lack of stories about the miserable quality and meager quantity of steamer chow:[49]

Barnum was traveling once on board of one of the river steamers, where they feed you for a moderate outlay (seventy-five cents a meal) very sumptuously, but the portions supplied were usually of microscopic dimensions. He called at tea-time for a beef-steak. The negro brought him the usual little, shriveled mite of boiled flesh, certainly not sufficient for more than two mouthfuls. Barnum poised the morsel on his fork, scanned it critically, as though it were a sample of steak submitted to his inspection, and then returned it to the waiter, saying, "Yes, that's what I mean. Bring me some of that."

Even during the late years of the steamboat traffic on the great rivers of the west, arrivals at the town docks were a matter of excitement and curiosity. Just as people today still like to watch airplanes coming and going, to and from exotic places of the world, so also did our pioneer ancestors gather at the river banks to watch the unloading and loading of exotic passengers and cargo. The first steamboats on the Missouri roused a certain amount of understandable terror among the Plains Indian villages along the river—and among others too:[50]

Sometime in the spring of '57 the steamer St. Nicholas "opened" in this city with a calliope—the first one ever heard in these parts—causing the greatest consternation among the servants, most of whom supposed they must now give an account of their sins, sure enough. But one of them stood and listened for some time, and at last expressed her opinion thus, "Missus, I don't believe dat ar's Gabriel, 'cause I ain't feard a bit; but if it is him, he's playin' 'Wait for the Wagon,' sure's you're born!"

Some idea of the state of safety standards on the river can be seen in this cartoon from the *Harpers Weekly* for February 27, 1858.[51] It was labeled "Portrait of a famous steamboat commodore, taken at the moment he was told that Congress was going to oblige steamers to carry lifeboats to save their passengers in case of shipwreck."

But if the Missouri seemed a peculiar river, the Platte, which served as the roadway for the thousands of travelers on the Oregon Trail moving to the Colorado and California gold fields or Oregon farmlands as well as the Mormon Trailers on their way to the Salt Lake, scarcely seemed like a river at all and almost demanded a new word for adequate description. It is not at all surprising that in a story related above it was referred to as "The Great Mirage":[52]

> The Platte resembled no river any of the emigrants had ever seen before, contradicting their idea of a "nor-

mal" stream. It was miles wide, and inches deep; thanks to Indian-set prairie fires and grazing buffalo, no timber grew on its banks; and it seemed to flow almost higher than the surrounding country. This phenomenon of an inverted river was noted by Alonzo Delano, who was rather mystified that the "Platte seemed to flow through higher ground than the tributaries of the Kansas. . . ." Exclaimed Martha Missouri Moore, "The river is a perfect curiosity, it is so very different from any of our streams that it is hard to realize that a river should be running so near the top of the ground without any timber, and no bank at all."

Not only is the river perversely high, shallow, and wide, but it was also accused by travelers of being upside down—"sand on the top, water underneath"—and backwards, for the narrowest part of its valley is its mouth, widening upstream from less than a mile wide to several score.

There is scarcely a book about early life on the Plains that does not describe them in nautical terms, like a sea of grass, the hills like ocean swells, not a book or collection of poems that does not speak of the Plains as the end of the earth, the rim of the world. So many things that had seemed so matter of course were gone here: farmers who had spent their lives fighting trees and rocks found none here, settlers who had fled troublesome neighbors ached for the sight of another face. Migrants found that they would now travel as far to a hardware store as they had previously traveled to foreign countries:[53]

A Nebraska paper complains bitterly of the mail's delays. Says the editor, "We received a letter two days ago from Chicago, informing us that its author would be in Nebraska last September. And since it was written he has been here, remained a month, made a thousand dollars in cash, had two fights, and had gone back and got married."

One of the first impressions Old Jules Sandoz, a Swiss, had of the Plains was violence. Few visitors could resist commenting on the fragility of the peace and the easy proximity of death that the frontiersman enjoyed: The standard reply if one asked about a departed soul, "Was it sudden?" was

"Well, rather sudden for him." A "Dakota flush" in poker was understood to be three jacks and a bowie knife, and Smith and Jones became inordinately universal names. In the East newspapers regaled readers with stories of the harsh life and even harsher death adventurers might expect for themselves out here, beyond civilization:[54]

> Bishop Vail of Kansas tells a little tale that illustrates forcibly the free-and-easy way of life of the frontiersman, and the scant ceremony with which his funeral services are conducted. "In one little graveyard where I happened to be walking," said the Bishop, "there were twenty-seven graves, and my informant, who discharged the office of undertaker, told me that the occupants of twenty-six of them were killed in affrays, or, as he pithily expressed it, died and were buried *with their boots on*." The twenty-seventh grave was that of a child.

Far more common and feared however, especially by the travelers on the Oregon and Mormon Trails, were the diseases that might be picked up at a water hole or from a casual brush with another, afflicted wagon train. Cholera could strike so quickly that a traveler who appeared happy and well at breakfast might be mourned by his widow at noon, and she by her orphaned children by nightfall.

Yet even the sicknesses had to serve their terms as the butts of pioneer humor:[55]

> There is an ailment, formerly more prevalent in this propinquity than at present, entitled fever and ague. It quivered and fluttered through our persons in a pleasant sort of way, just enough to remind us of our quinine. Compared with the manner it takes hold of one in the West, it is a mere bagatelle. Its perfect development seems to have been reached in Arkansas, judging from the following description given by an expert between whiffs from his pipe: "Maybe ye'll get some idea of the Arkansaw ager when I tell ye that I once unjinted both shoulders in shakin', and it was a light shake at that. When I had one of my regular double-back-action shakes, I could jar a jug of whiskey out of the crotch of a tree twenty-eight rods off. Nobody dast pile up cord-wood within half a mile of my cabin, and that's a solemn fact. I devoured kyneen [quinine] just as you eat corned beef,

and my hull system finally got so bitter that a dog who smelled of my leg couldn't get the pucker out of his mouth inside of ten days. Gentlemen, I do not wish to prolong this agony. We will have some licker, and I will then seek a few needed reposes."

Foodways too changed as a result of the diminished and restricted supplies and one either adjusted to those changes or went hungry. The most widely told story about life on the state lines crossing the Plains was retold in one of its many variations in the pages of *Harpers New Monthly Magazine*, in the column known as the "Editor's Drawer," in April of 1865:[56]

At a station on the overland route the keeper got rather short of provisions—in fact, had nothing left but a bottle of mustard and some bacon. As the stage stopped there one day to change horses the passengers seated themselves at the table and the host said, "Shall I help you to a piece of bacon?"

"No, thank you; I never eat bacon," said one traveler.

"Well, then," said the station-keeper, "help yourself to the mustard."

That the drinks were also something less than vintage stock is suggested by labels like "skull varnish," "Injun killer," "popskull," and stories like the one about the new Westerner who was asked if the stuff he was drinking in his new home was anything like the good stuff he used to get "back home." "Well, I don't know," he replied, thinking the matter over carefully, "I guess so. There is only one queer thing about it; whenever I wipe my mouth I burn a hole in my shirt."[57]

Speaking of booze, I think the most remarkable triple entendre I have encountered thus far in my work with American pioneer humor is this—[58]

"Josh, does the sun ever rise in the West?"

"Never."

"Never?"

"Never."

"You don't say so! Well, you won't get me to emigrate to the West, if it's always night there. I have a cousin who is ever boasting how pleasant it is in that region, but it must be all moonshine."

Improvisation had long been a standard quality of pioneer American culture but in the West it reached new limits—and went beyond them:[59]

> A young man went from New York City to the West, where he commenced business on his own account, and married. His friends in the City were interested in his welfare, and when a merchant was about to journey to the place where the young man had located, he was requested to visit the emigrant and ascertain how he lived, what sort of wife he had chosen, his prospects, etc. Accordingly, the New Yorker ascertained the residence of his young friend and called upon him quite early in the morning. He found him in a small cottage, and just taking his breakfast. The introduction of the New Yorker to his wife was quite offhand and unceremonious and he was requested to be seated, and partake of the morning meal. The young wife had prepared the steak, biscuit, and coffee with her own hands, and for a table had used her kneading board placed on her lap. The New Yorker declined a seat at the table, and took his leave. On making his report to his New York friends as to how he found his young friend living, he described the style as "magnificent!" and for explanation of the superlative he said, that were he the owner of that young man's furniture, he would not take ten thousand dollars for the legs of his table.

The riches hoped for by the migrants and promised them by the speculators were only rarely amassed and a substantial proportion of the Plains tall tales and other forms of humor dwell on the poverty and hardships of the frontier. Perhaps the most telling remarks were those like, "When I came out here I didn't have a rag on my back. But now here I am: covered with rags."[60] And a variation on that theme:[61]

> Apropos of mining in the Black Hills, a young man of Williamsport, Pennsylvania, who went there to seek his fortune, and wrote back to his father that he had done well, added this P.S. "I will be home on Wednesday evening. Meet me at dark, just out of town, and bring a

blanket or a whole pair of trousers with you. I *have* a hat."

The land exacted its toll all right. The *Ainsworth Journal* of Brown County, Nebraska,[62] reported in 1885 that when the cry went up, "Let everybody shout for his own country," Nebraskans were known to burst out with an enthusiastic, "Hurrah for Hell!" and the same issue of that paper observed that " . . . the following suggestive lines were found on the door of a dugout in the Sandhills[63] in the southern part of Brown County last week:

"250 feet to water,
50 miles to fuel,
6 inches to Hell,
God bless, our home!"

I especially admire the placement of that comma in the last line!

Those who scoff today at the label "Great American Desert" need read only a few pioneer accounts to understand that those who came here to the Plains and lived on the land came expecting to find a desert and were seldom disappointed. If the land did eventually become a gardenland, they felt that it was by virtue of their toil and courage rather than the gracious benevolence of the Plains. An early observer put it quite nicely, I think, when he wrote in 1877,[64] "Finally this enlightener takes his slippered feet inside the railroad car and sums up thus, 'Nebraska and Hell lack the same thing—good society and water.' " I was told about a farm that I bought near Dannebrog, Nebraska, that the soil was so bad that I would be lucky to raise my voice on it, and another observer noted that it would be hard to raise hell there, even given a gallon of good whiskey.

In most areas of Europe and the Eastern area of the United States, from which so many of the Plains frontier migrants came, two primary problems of agriculture were trees and rocks. Before a farm could be tilled it was necessary to cut down the huge hardwoods and then grub out the roots; for years thereafter the yeoman had to fight the new saplings every spring. As the plow cut across the field he would stop every few steps to free the plowshare from a root or to pick up a rock and throw it to the edge of the field, where there grew over the years a veritable stone wall. On the Plains frontier that problem was nonexistent. On the other hand, all of the things that those stones and wood had been used for now had to be fabricated from other materials—or done without.

The hazards were met, as usual, with humor. Edward Everett Dale recorded a tale that played on the perverse nature of the Plains:[65]

> . . . An old gentleman from the wooded hills of Tennessee once paid a visit to his two nephews who were ranching on the plains of western Texas. The two young men met him at the nearest railroad point with a spring wagon and camping outfit and the trio set out in the early afternoon for the ranch some seventy miles distant. A little before sundown they stopped to make camp near a windmill that stood not far from the banks of a dry, sandy arroyo which meandered across the level prairie. One of the young men took a pick axe from the wagon and began digging in the dry earth nearby from which grew a few mesquite sprouts.

> Soon he had unearthed an armful of large mesquite roots, brought them to the wagon and kindled a fire. In the meantime his brother had unharnessed the horses, watered them at the big circular metal stock tank beside the windmill and staked them out to graze on the thick buffalo grass. He then seized an iron pail and hung it over the end of the iron pipe leading from the windmill to the stock tank. There was not a breath of air stirring but the young man climbed the steel ladder leading to the top of the windmill tower and turned the great wheel with his hands until a stream of fresh, clear water poured from the pipe and filled the pail. Returning to the campfire, he filled the coffeepot and began to prepare supper.

> The old uncle who had been sitting on the wagon tongue watching these proceedings with a jaundiced eye but considerable interest suddenly inquired: "Is there ever any water in that creek?" "Oh, yes," was the answer, "when it rains and for a few days or weeks afterward." "What's the name of it anyhow?" continued the old man. "Jose Creek," answered the nephew, "J-o-s-e, pronounced hosay." The old man snorted indignantly: "I don't know why you boys want to stay out here. I wouldn't live in

any country where you have to climb for water, and dig for wood, and spell hell with a J!"

So it was that experienced Plains homesteaders noted that "No woman should live in this country who cannot climb a windmill or shoot a gun," or "On the Plains the wind draws the water and the cows cut the wood."[66] So it was that the word "hell" was so often associated with the Plains:

> "This," said the newcomer to the Plains, "would be a fine country if we just had water."
>
> "Yes," answered the man whose wagon tongue pointed east, "So would Hell."

Some conditions on the Plains were intensified versions of geographical features that might be found elsewhere, but others were uniquely products of the Plains and occur, so far as I know, nowhere else on earth:[67]

> Professor Daniel T. Wright of St. Louis passed through St. Joseph today on route to Fremont, Nebraska, where he will secure a tram and proceed 120 miles north of there to examine a huge boulder that is one of the greatest curiousities of the present age. It is nothing less than a huge magnet that is powerful enough to attract animals and men to it and hold them fast. Three weeks ago a man living some ten miles from the rock went hunting. During the morning of the second day a heavy rain came up and he was thoroughly soaked. He started for home and happened to come across the rock. As he approached it he saw a rabbit which appeared to be crouching on the side of the rock.
>
> The rain was pouring down and it appeared funny that a rabbit should be in such an exposed position and his curiousity being aroused he approached the rock to investigate. The rabbit made no attempt to run away and when the hunter stepped near and was in the act of reaching for the animal he was astonished to feel his gun trying to pull out of his hands. He then felt himself being irresistibly drawn toward the rock and before he could comprehend his danger found himself and gun stuck tight against the boulder from which he could not pull himself away. His hands and wet clothing clung to the wet rock and it was not long before he began to realize what the trouble was. He knew at once that he would not be able

to escape until it quit raining and dried off, and he doubted very much whether he could then. About 1 o'clock the rain subsided and the sun came out. By 4 o'clock his garments were dry, and as they no longer acted as a conductor he was able to move himself away but did not succeed until after summoning all of his strength he gave a herculean wrench and breaking his hold fell headlong away from the boulder. His gun, however, and the rabbit still clung tenaciously thereto, and he was compelled to go away and leave them. He reported his strange discovery and several have already visited the scene and confirmed all he said about the rock. Professor Wright is a learned geologist and will test the natural magnet thoroughly when he arrives there.

One of the problems in imagining what the Plains frontier was like for those who experienced it is inventorying and sensing those things that we today take for granted that then were strange and exotic phenomena—for example, cactus. Bill Nye, the best of western humorists, was clearly well acquainted with cacti and sensitive to their most impressive points, as it were:[68]

He . . . had some Western cactus as a curiosity for the tenderfoot who had never fooled with cactus much.

It was the clear thing however. I sat down on one to test its genuineness. It stood the test better than I did. When you have doubts about a cactus and don't know whether it is a genuine cactus or a young watermelon with its hair banged, you can test it by sitting down on it. It may surprise you at first, but it tickles the cactus almost to death. . . .

It is very easy to live, and don't require much fondling. It will enjoy life better if you will get mad at it about once a week and pull it up by the roots, and kick it around the yard. Water it carefully every four years; if you water it oftener than that, it will be surprised, and gradually pine away and die.

Another item I must not forget in giving directions for the cultivation of this rare tropical plant; get someone to sit down on it occasionally—if you don't feel equal to it yourself. There's nothing that makes a cactus thrive and flourish so much as to have a victim with linen pants on, sit down on it and then get up impulsively like. If a cactus can have these little attentions bestowed upon it, it will live to a good old age, and insinuate itself through the pantaloons of generations yet unborn. Plant in a gravelly, coarse soil, and kick it every time you think of it.

I would have demanded however that Nye, had I ever had the good fortune to meet him, admit that Plains summers have no parallels in the Rockies and Wyoming cactus is as dangerous as a puffball in comparison with Plains sandburs and puncture vine. Furthermore, Nye's descriptions of the poverty and hard times he experienced in Colorado and Wyoming mining camps are so niggling in comparison with Plains tales of the same kinds of joys that his pathetic accounts are viewed as thin-blooded jokes by contemporary Plainsmen.

A Nebraska farmer, for example, once told me of talking with a discouraged neighbor and asking him, by way of lightening the conversation, what he would do if he had a million dollars. "Why," came the reply, "Apply it to my debts, as far as it'd go."

The same broken man finally left the Plains and farming because, he said, he got damned tired of hearing his corn-picking machine say "Here's one! Here's one!"

A distinguished Lincoln, Nebraska, matron told me that she had not always been so comfortably situated and added by way of proof that she had been eighteen years old before she realized that Gooches Flour Mill made anything other than underwear.

She also told me that a terrible physical handicap had kept her and her sisters from finding suitable husbands until they were well into their twenties. She paused long enough for my curiosity and sympathy to develop fully and then explained, "We had each developed a huge, hooked toe on our right feet from turning over cowchips to see if they were dry enough to use as fuel, and Pa couldn't afford to buy the shoes to cover those toes up."

"Cow wood" or "Nebraska Oak" was for many years the standard fuel on the Plains and few women of that period ever overcame their revulsion enough to be able to laugh at the situation as this lady did.[69]

Even where there was legitimate, real wood, its lumber didn't behave like civilized wood:[70]

"I had a dog once, back in Nebraska, that I kept to herd lumber. It was this way. Cottonwood boards warp like thunder in the sun. A board would begin to hump its back up about nine in the morning, and in half an hour, it would turn over. By eleven it would warp the other way with the heat, and make another flop. Each time it turned it moved a couple of feet, always following the sun towards the west. The first summer I lived in Brownville over 10,000 feet of lumber skipped out to the hills the day before I had advertised a house raisin'. I went to the county seat to attend a lawsuit and when I got back there wasn't a stick of timber left. It had strayed away into the uplands. An ordinary board would climb a two-mile hill during a hot week, and when it struck the timber it would keep wormin' in and out among the trees like a garter snake. Every farmer in the state had to keep shepherd dogs to follow his lumber around the country, keep it together, and show where it was in the morning. We didn't need any flumes there for lumber. We sawed it east of the place we wanted to use it, and let it warp itself to its destination, with men and dogs to head it off at the right time, and we never lost a stick. Well, here comes the jury," continued the judge. "The witnesses lied, so I guess they will disagree."

Life was indeed hard, what with the perversity of the weather, the hard times, and everything else conspiring to defeat the hardy homesteader. Conditions of abject poverty and drouth revisited the Plains during the Dirty Thirties and so did the jokes about the hard times. One of my father's favorites told of a newspaper salesman during the Depression years who had just finished a particularly disastrous day and resolved to sell at least one subscription before he called it a day, no matter what it took. He entered a farmer's yard and hailed him as he left the barn. "How about a subscription to the newspaper?" the salesman asked. "I'll take whatever money you happen to have."

"Ain't got any money," replied the ragged farmer.

"Well, I'll take a couple of dozen eggs then."

"Sold the chickens."

"Then I'll take a few quarts of milk or a couple pounds of butter."

"Sold the cows."

"I'll settle for a couple bushel of corn then."

"Shelled the corn and sold it all."

"Okay, last offer: I'll take a load of cobs for a subscription."

"Listen, mister, I cain't read and if I had cobs I wouldn't need your newspaper."

Regretfully, not all of the problems of the Plains were caused by the tough geography. Indeed, a good part of the agony of the Dustbowl was caused by man's own abuse of the land that had been so good to him, that had been so precious. As one joke of the period summarized it,[71] "Don't tell me how to farm," an old-timer said to a new, young college-educated county extension agent. "I've already worn out eight farms just by myself."

I will close this recitation of the agonies of Plains pioneer life with a poem, published in the *Harpers New Monthly Magazine* in 1869[72], which suggests that life in the city was not much more attractive than life in the grasslands. It was introduced in the *Magazine* with the single sentence, "A gentleman who was smitten with the Overland-Omaha-Pacific-Railroad-California fever is incited to describe in disgustful poesy his impressions of that objectionable region."

> Hast ever been to Omaha,
>   Where rolls the dark Missouri down,
> And four strong horses scarce can draw
>   An empty wagon through the town?
>
> Where sand is blown from every mound,
>   To fill your eyes and ears and throat;
> Where all the steamers are aground,
>   And all the shanties are afloat?
>
> Where whisky-shops the livelong night
>   Are vending out their poison-juice,
> Where men are often *very* tight,
>   And women deemed a trifle loose?

Where taverns have an anxious guest
  For every corner, shelf, and crack;
With half the people going West,
  And *all* the others going back?

Where theatres are all the run,
  And bloody scalpers come to trade;
Where everything is overdone
  And everybody underpaid?

If not, take heed to what I say;
  You'll find it just as I have found it;
And if it lies upon your way,
  For God's sake, reader, *go around it*!

2

JUST SUMMER
AND WINTER

God, but it looks like rain.
                    Anonymous graffito scratched on a wall of
            abandoned potash works in Antioch, Nebraska

This is crazy weather; I'm going to invent a straw hat with
ear flaps.
                    Frank Mejstrik, West Point, Nebraska

"Think it's going to rain?"
"Be a long dry spell if it don't."
                    Standard Plains exchange

Ashes to ashes, and dust to dust,
The menfolks raved and the wimmin cussed.
Take it and like it; in God we trust.
                    Anonymous graffito scratched on dusty window
                        of abandoned homestead shack in Kansas

In his book *The Great Platte River Road* Merrill Mattes
captures part of the agony of those who crossed the Plains
on the Oregon and Mormon Trails:[1]

> Thunder and lightning, hail, hurricane, or tornado
> were more spectacular, but the most demoralizing and all-
> pervading enemy was rain. True, it made the essential
> grass grow, but one could be miserably wet and come
> close to drowning in it. The young tenderfoot learned in
> a hurry about digging a ditch around the tent to divert
> ground water. But a ditch six feet deep would scarcely
> keep out some Platte River cloudbursts. . . . Storm-
> bound at Fort Kearny, Meline explained his dilemma:

"You can't lie down without being drowned or stand up without being struck by lightning."

But it is not altogether accurate that the worst element of the weather was rain. The worst feature of the weather was that one which happened to be afflicting the victim at any particular time. Now it was the rain, now it was the heat:

"Wow! Did you hear? It's 110° in the shade."
"Then stay out of the shade."

Of course it's an old joke. That's the point. It is old and has survived because it says so well how futile it was to try to resist.

Plains weather has been the focus of an inordinate amount of humor because it constantly occupied the mind of the Plains pioneer. As a farmer he knew that the weather was his bread and butter. A good rain could bring him wealth, a sudden freeze could destroy him, and if he spent four seasons on the Plains he knew how fickle the weather could be. The absolute temperature range for the Plains, as I have mentioned above, is about 180°, the same difference as that between freezing and boiling. The largest hailstones recorded in the United States have fallen on the Plains. Incredibly rapid temperature changes boggle the mind as well as the wardrobe. On February 29, 1972, it was 89° in Lincoln, Nebraska, and I found myself in the peculiar situation, while trying out the new canoe I had received for Christmas, of sweating shirtless under a merciless sun while struggling to haul my canoe over enormous ice floes. One Nebraska day my University classes were canceled because a snowstorm had brought the city to a complete halt. That afternoon I washed my car and that late afternoon I took my boat out sailing. Each action was appropriate to the weather of that moment.

The pioneer sensed these contradictions and extremes even more than we might because they were more important to him and he lacked the moderating machinery of good, automotive heating and cooling systems and a versatile and extensive set of clothing. Which may explain experiences like the following:[2]

It was my pleasure to know this 'old-timer who settled long ago in Nebraska. His background is rich in lore and tradition and his experiences many and some a trifle spectacular. . . .

One day in May he decided to plant some corn and so proceeded to the south field to start operations. It being dreadfully warm he paused for a rest not far from the end of the field.

Suddenly a buck deer leaped from cover and took off. Ananias immediately abandoned his outfit and gave chase. But the deer for some reason or another outdistanced him, jumped the fence, and disappeared.

Ananias, of course, was disgruntled at this but ran on, mostly to reassure himself that the deer had escaped. This might sound silly to some who did not know him but he had (so he said) caught plenty of deer afoot.

Imagine his great surprise—likewise gratification—when he discovered the deer securely trapped in a huge snowbank just beyond the fence!

This brought to his memory the time he pursued an elk with horns six feet wide from point to point through their pasture timber where the trees grew only two or three feet apart. He lost that one however as the elk was a little too fast for him.

That summer was so hot that this ten-acre field of popcorn he planted that May day all popped and the result was so stupendous that Mountain bound tourists all flocked there, thinking they had reached the snow-covered peaks of the Rockies.

To further confuse these travelers another little incident occurred at the same time. It seems there was a large ice house and ice pond near Ananias' farm. This had been used so much for putting up ice that some unusual conditions had brought about the formation of immense ice caverns underneath the lake and ice house.

Perhaps induced by the vibration from the popping corn, this subterranean formation began to erupt millions of tons of ice, a frigid volcano, so to speak, which upheaved such mountains of ice that the popcorn high peaks were really dwarfed. So swift was the action of this strange eruption that the intense heat was changed to sub-zero temperature and froze everything for miles around, including a few sightseers.

That winter which followed was the worst ever, said Ananias. He attempted to take a bath one night and so filled a tub with scalding hot water. Having part of a pail left over he carelessly threw it out of the window. It froze before it reached the ground and killed their best watchdog. The ice was still too hot to touch. Climbing into the tub of scalding water, Ananias suddenly found himself encased in ice, which was so hot he was badly burned.

However, being a patient soul, he waited until another spring rolled around and then managed to extricate himself before the ice became heated up from the severe summer weather.

It is worth noting that the above narrator has combined in this single passage tales of extreme heat, extreme cold, and violent change. It is worth noting because it is a severe but faithful reflection of truth. It is the same geography which allows stories like these—[3]

Violent climatic changes brought forth a whole new set of stories about life on the plains. Kansans obliged to endure unbelievably hot summers, solemnly swore that when their sinners passed away they were buried in overcoats to keep them warm when they reached the cooler region of Hell. . . .

that also made room for tales like this—[4]

It was so cold that the milk would freeze before it would hit the bottom of the bucket, so we would just milk over our arm until we had an armload of frozen squirts which we would then take into the house and melt as we needed them.

Within the genre of the tall tale there is a range of intensities. The bulk of them, and thus those reflecting most clearly the true (so to speak) nature of the "tall tale," incorporates exaggerations so gross that no one is ever deceived. Indeed the humor rests precisely on the outrageous nature of the exaggeration:[5]

It was so cold we had to build a fire under the cow to melt the milk in the udder.

Others are too close to the truth for comfort; it is clear that the editor commenting on this item believed it to be a tall-tale exaggeration and yet many ranchers know all too well that Sam Gregg's story was probably true—brutally, painfully true:[6]

> Sam Gregg, who is up in Holt County [Nebraska], writes that there are 80,000 cattle standing up to the hay stacks in the upper country, frozen to death. Sam will be remembered by our old Nimrods as the individual who once had hold of an eight hundred pound pickerel in Jacksons Lake about ten years ago. His reputation for truth and veracity may therefore be relied upon.

But the most pathetic dimension of the tall tale were those fantasies that were believed by the homesteaders themselves—sad, hopeful delusions that gave some chance that what they could see was true was somehow itself an exaggeration. Perhaps, they told themselves, the very plowing of the ground will cause there to be more rain, but there wasn't. Perhaps the trees would bring the rain, but they didn't. If it was impossibly cold last winter, then it should be cooler next summer, but it was hotter:[7]

> Old theories about the extreme cold and extended droughts were discounted. The chamber-of-commerce spirit now took over, and newly arrived homesteaders in the Dakotas told each other that it was good for the ground to freeze to such unusual depths—it arrested the evaporation of water and stored it for spring needs.

Curiously, even in pioneer years the old-timers would tell of the older times when things were tougher and people more resilient:[8]

> One of the most interesting storytellers in Brownville [Nebraska] is Hugh Baker. The frosts of many winters have whitened his head, but his heart is still sunny. The present cold spell recalls one of his reminiscences.
>
> "Boys," said he, on one occasion, "You don't know nothing about cold weather. I can remember one year when it was so cold here that I walked across the river on the ice to Scott City, Missouri, where I got some whiskey. It was frozen in chunks and I carried it in my handkerchief. On my arrival in Brownville I gave a piece of it to each one of my friends and they had to break the chunks with their hatchets in order to thaw it out so they could drink it."

The editor of the *Arapahoe* [Nebraska] *Pioneer* was interested enough to initiate a serious investigation of earlier cold temperatures on the Plains, temperatures for which, apparently, records no longer exist:[9]

> We have examined our chronology and find that the winter of 1880 has not by any means been the coldest one. In 1831 it was so cold that boiling water froze stiff over the red-hot fire. In 1827 oil froze in the lamps and people had no lights until spring set in. In 1821 it was so cold that people breathed hard, let it freeze, cut a hole in it, and crawled in for shelter.
>
> In 1817 people wore undershirts of sandpaper to keep up friction. In 1813 it was so cold that smoke froze in the chimneys and it had to be blasted out with dynamite. In . . . but the fate of Ananias and Sapphira looms up before us and we rest.

The editor was wise to break off that narrative. For those who might have forgotten Acts: 5-10, the story of Ananias and his wife Sapphira, I will include the Biblical passage here as a fine lesson for anyone tempted to tell untruths:

> . . . A man named Ananias with his wife Sapphira sold a piece of property, and with his wife's knowledge he kept back some of the proceeds, and brought only a part and laid it at the apostle's feet. But Peter said, "Ananias, why has Satan filled your heart to lie to the Holy Spirit and to keep back part of the proceeds of the land? While it remained unsold, did it not remain your own? And after it was sold, was it not at your disposal? How is it that you have contrived this deed in your heart? You have not lied to men but to God." When Ananias heard these words, he fell down and died. And shortly thereafter, when his wife heard the words, she died too.

As I get older the winters do indeed seem to get colder and longer. I took great solace recently when the *Omaha World-Herald* reported[10] that the editor of the Stanton, Nebraska, *Register*[11] had observed, ". . . we used to brag about our Nebraska spring and fall weather but lately it has become only hot or cold. Some wag said Nebraska's seasons have changed to 1) summer, 2) get ready for winter, 3) winter, 4) get over winter."

Now I thought that was a pretty fair line—until I ran across the acid essay by Bill Nye entitled "Sitting Down on a Venerable Joke":[12]

Near St. Paul, on the Sioux City road, I met the very present man from Leadville again. I had met him before on every division of every railroad I had traveled over but I nodded to him, and he began to tell me all about Leadville [South Dakota].

He saw that I looked sad, and he cheered me up with little prehistoric jokes that an antiquarian had given him years ago. Finally he said, "Leadville is mighty cold; it has such an all-fired altitude. The summer is very short and unreliable, and the winter long and severe.

"An old miner over in California Gulch got off a pretty good joke about the climate there. A friend asked him about the seasons at Leadville, and he said that there they had nine months winter and three months late in the fall."

Then he looked around to see me fall to pieces with mirth, but I restrained myself and said, "You will please excuse me for not laughing at that joke. I cannot do it. It is too sacred.

"Do you think I would laugh at the bones of the Pilgrim Fathers, where are they? or burst into wild hilarity over the grave of Noah and his family?

"No sir; their age and antiquity protect them. That is the way with your Phoenician joke.

"Another reason why I cannot laugh at it is this: I am not a very easy and extemporaneous laugher anyway. I am generally shrouded in gloom especially when I am in hot pursuit of a wild and skittish joke for my own use. It takes a good, fair, average joke that hasn't been used much to make me laugh easy, and besides, I have used up the fund of laugh that I had laid aside for that particular joke. It has, in fact, overdrawn some now, and is behind.

"I do not wish to intrench on that fund that I have concluded to offer as a purse for young jokes that have never made it in three minutes.

"I want to encourage green jokes, too, that have never trotted in harness before, and besides, I must insist on using my scanty fund of laugh on jokes of the nineteenth century. I have got to draw the line somewhere.

"If I were making a collection of antique jokes of the vintage of 1400 years B.C., or arranging and classifying little *bon mots* of the time of Cleopatra or King Solomon, I would give you a handsome sum for this one of yours, but I am just trying to worry along and pay expenses, and trying to be polite to everyone I meet, and laughing at lots of things that I don't want to laugh at, and I am going to quit it.

"That is why I have met your little witticism with cold and heartless gravity."

Despite such righteous indignation, Nye himself was capable of telling some stories of vintage and his accounts were sometimes the targets of accusations of falsehood. On one occasion he and some companions were caught in a sudden snowstorm while traveling between Wyoming gold camps. According to him,[13] the snowflakes ". . . came sauntering through the air like pure, white Turkish towels falling from the celestial clotheslines." After a long hard struggle, during which the constant fear was that they would die alone in the woods, they finally made it to clear land, were picked up and returned safely to their homes. Nye concluded, "We may learn from this a valuable lesson, but at this moment I do not know exactly what it is."

The ingenuity that is so much of the American's reputation and salvation could meet the challenge of even this kind of weather threat, if this report of January 30, 1877, from the Fremont [Nebraska] *Daily Herald* is to be trusted:[14]

One of the dozen passengers on a Woodware Ave. car suddenly remarked that it was an awful snowstorm and that he never saw so much snow on the ground before.

"Pooh!" exclaimed a little whiffet of a man in the corner; "This is no snowstorm at all! Why, in Omaha I have seen forty-seven feet of snow on the ground at once."

"Buried the town, didn't it?" queried the man opposite.

"Of course it buried the town, but that was all right. We dug out the snow and left a crust, as a sort of sky, and in three days we had summer weather down there. Roses bloomed, peach trees blossomed, and the boys went swimming, the same as in July. Don't talk to me about such storms as this!"

"What became of the crust?" gasped the man at the front end of the car.

"It is hanging there yet," replied the noble liar, "and the man who doubts my word wants to step off the car for a half minute."

One of my favorite contemporary storytellers is Ray Harpham of Holstein, Nebraska. In a letter to me dated March 8, 1976, he told a story that makes me believe that the spirit of the hardy pioneers, not to mention the spirit of hardy pioneer winters, is nowhere near gone:

I had quite an experience in last November nineteenth's blizzard, and I thought you might be interested in it. Fact is I am just now getting out of my rocking chair and back on my feet—I never lie.

I was out cutting some trees and got caught in the blizzard. I was carrying the chainsaw and that saved my life. it was snowing so hard and blowing so much I couldn't quite get anywhere. Was that snow thick! I started up the saw and cut a bunch of blocks out of it and made an igloo. It wasn't bad in there but I didn't have anything to eat with me. Quick thinking saved me again. I figured that if anyone ever had the wolf at the door I did, so I drug him in and ate him—all but the howl. I froze that and sawed it up in pieces and have it in my deep freezer. I am thawing them out now and I usually use them when the news comes on but the rest of them I'll save for the campaign speeches this fall. It beats listening to all that hot air.

I sure am glad to be alive and able to report this to you. For some reason people seem to believe you more than they do me. If you should doubt this story I can prove it by the tooth marks on my chainsaw.

Yours very truly [!]
Ray Harpham

Spring rains could be just as destructive as the snows when given the chance. A Rising City, Nebraska, newspaper noted in 1877:[15]

A fragment of Bill Nye's forty liars has settled down

to business in Butler County [Nebraska]. The Rising City *Independent* reports the proceedings thus: "During that heavy rain we had a few weeks ago," said a farmer living southwest of town, "I put a barrel out by the barn and it was filled with rainwater in just ten minutes by the watch."

"That's nothing," remarked Gillis Doty, who was standing near chewing a straw. "I put a barrel out in my yard during the same shower, that had both heads out, and blamed if the rain didn't go through the bunghole so fast that it couldn't run out at the ends and overflowed at the bung!"

Fog always seems too ephemeral to me to count as real precipitation, but I think that this story about fog belongs right here, along with the rain and snow tales, because it appears to have had substance enough to pass the test. It was reported in the *Harpers New Monthly Magazine* of January, 1864,[16] that there was a fog out west of Chicago that was so bad that a train engineer could not see the length of his engine. He told his conductor that he did not intend to be held responsible if any cows were killed that day because he simply could not handle a fog of that density. He claimed that he had to bore a hole through the fog with an auger to see anything at all, and "When I drew my head back [from the fog], there was a round hole left where I put out my head!"

A South Dakota folklorist, Dorothy Shonsey, was once told about a similar fog condition:[17]

> The fog would get so thick in Nebraska that the Indians would nearly starve to death. [They] would sneak up on a buffalo and when they shot the arrow it would stick in the fog.

Of course the same farmers who complained and cursed the heavens when there was no rain, complained and cursed the sky when it did rain, probably because it was always a case of too much of either and/or both:[18]

> An egotistical friend of ours—who believes himself at the same time the center, the object, and the cause of everything that exists, and everything that takes place, said to us the other day, "It is only to me that such misfortunes happen!"

"What is the matter?" we asked.
"Don't you see that it is raining?" he answered.

I felt like that once, legitimately. I was engaged to be the speaker for a "rural appreciation night" in Franklin, Nebraska. A "rural appreciation night" is an occasion when the merchants of a small town invite their best farm customers to town for a free banquet and some cheap entertainment, which on this occasion was me. I closed my program of Plains pioneer folksongs and tales by singing "Sweet Nebraska Land":[19]

Ah Nebraska Land, sweet Nebraska Land,
As on thy burning soil I stand,
I look away across the Plains
And wonder why it never rains.

We've reached the land of desert sweet
Where nothing grows for man to eat,
And the wind it blows with fev'rish heat
Across these plains so hard to beat.

We have no wheat, we have no oats,
We have no corn to feed our shoats;
Our chickens are so very poor,
They beg for crumbs outside the door.

Our horses are of bronco race;
Starvation stares them in the face.
We do not live, we only stay,
'Cause we're too poor to move away.

As I sang this pioneer song of the "desert sweet," I was standing in front of a wall of windows and behind me the rain was lashing against the panes as it had been doing for weeks. The farmers were wearing irrigation boots, which they had had to wear so that they could plod through the mud of the barnyard to the tractor, which they had had to use to get to their cars sitting on the road—the farm roads were totally impassable. I apologized for the embarrassing inappropriateness of the song, but explained that this was the way the pioneers had sung it after all.

After my presentation a farmer came up to me and called my attention to the fact that I had just finished telling them tall tales that expressed both extremes—the hot and the cold, the drought and the flood—and, he explained, that is the way it had been with that song too. And he sang me verses which I have prized ever since:

Ah Nebraska Land, Sweet Nebraska Land,
As on thy sodden soil I stand,
I look away across the Plains
And pray to God to stop the rains.

We have no wheat, we have no oats,
We cannot harvest them in boats;
Our chickens are too poor to eat;
They have no webs upon their feet.

Our horses are of bronco race,
They have to swim from place to place;
We do not live, we only stay,
We have no boats to move away.

But with a smile upon our lips
We stand in mud up to our hips;
Nebraska Land, so fertile and rich,
We think you are a . . . honey.

It is true that wet springs and falls were ever a hazard for frontier country where the roads were primitive and the conveyances considerably less than sophisticated, and songs like that above and stories like these below arose to provide the sustaining laughter to counter the conditions:[20]

Near the mouth of the Ohio are two rival cities which sometimes manage to keep their heads above water. The editors of both towns have been telling some queer stories about the late submerge. The Mound City *Emporium* is responsible for the subjoined dry joke on a wet subject: "The steamer *Manchester* has been engaged inside the levees at Cairo [Illinois], during a considerable portion the past week, towing houses from one point to another, and getting drift out of the town. The report that she tore part of her bottom off by running over the top of the Taylor house is without foundation."

"You have considerable floating population in this village, haven't you?" asked a stranger of one of the citizens of a village on the Mississippi.

"Well, rather," was the reply, "about half the year the water is up to the second-story windows."

Even when the water did not achieve the level of inundation it could cause consternation for the frontiersmen. A colleague once told me[21] that in his home area, during muddy springs, no one worried about the cattle as long as you could see their ears above the mud. Another depressed plainsman lamented[22] that the mud was so slippery in Nebraska that "you'd take one step forward and slip two back, so the only way you could ever get anywhere was to walk the other way."

But the real bulk of the stories and the real bulk of pioneer travails came not from too much rain but from too little. It is not surprising therefore that the humor in these stories seems especially biting. I have remarked before in these pages that the trees were so rare on the early Plains that they could serve as distinctive landmarks, not to be confused with any other, nearby trees because there were no other, nearby trees. In some decades the same was true of a good year, or a good season, or even one good rain. I was once told by an old-timer, who was trying to emphasize for me the intensity of 19th-century droughts, about a Nebraska farmer who was asked by a census taker when his son, a strapping young man, had been born. "That summer it rained," came the laconic reply. In Dannebrog, Nebraska, where I have a small farm, I heard the comment in Bob and Nora's Silver Dollar Bar that "In this country too much rain is just right" and that the summer before, it had been so dry that a local resident had seen two cottonwood trees fighting over a dog. Even during the winter there was no respite and last winter it was estimated that near Dannebrog some fields were running less than ten bushel of snow to the acre.

In some cases it is not so much the intensity of the dryness that is remarkable but the conditions that resulted from that dryness:[23]

A guy came out and the guy was standing there filling up gopher holes. Guy says, "What are you doing?" and he says, "I'm irrigating."

"Irrigating? What do you mean, irrigating?"

He says, "If I don't plug up these holes the wind blows so hard and it gets so hot that the water just evaporates up out of the ground through these gopher holes."

* * *

It was so hot in the summertime that the windmill would pump water so fast that it'd overflow the tanks, except the cows were so dry they'd drink the water faster than the windmill could pump it, except that when the cows were five, ten, fifteen years old they were all scared of drinking water because just as soon as the well went dry it'd blast sand right in their faces.

The results of the droughts were far reaching and staggering, and the solution for the resultant problems had to match them in presumption: a pioneer newspaper[24] reported in 1890 that it was so dry in its area that " . . . the farmers have to soak their hogs to make them hold swill and . . . the creek bottom is all warped out of shape and will have to be sprinkled and ironed."[25]

Nor did the advent of modern times and technology change the hardships:[26]

[A] pilot . . . was obliged to abandon his plane and after parachuting out had to spend six hours shoveling his way back to earth.

It was so dusty that when two road maintainers met they would throw a clod and talk through the hole.

No stories about heat and drought on the Plains are complete without accompanying stories about the wind. It is significant that of the twenty-one cities listed in the *New York Times 1970 Almanac* as having average wind speeds of over ten miles per hour, twelve are on the Plains, ten of them on the northern Plains. This is all the more impressive because so low a percentage of the total cities listed are on the Plains.

It is not surprising then that a newspaper like the Gering, Nebraska, *Courier*, situated only a few miles from the

Nebraska-Wyoming border, could print a story like this on December 22, 1893:[27]

> Charlie Ford has just been up in Wyoming and in speaking of the little prejudice those Cheyenne fellows have against Nebraska he said this section was a sweet boon when sized up with the country he saw. "Why," he said, "I saw one place up there where the soil was all blown away, and the prairie-dog holes were left sticking three feet and a half up in the air."

Anyone who is impressed by these weather reports— and who could help but be impressed by them?—must also be impressed by the brilliant tactic the pioneers used in turning their worst difficulties into their best advantages. During one particularly ferocious sandstorm in Nebraska's Sandhills country a crew of carpenters found that all they had to do was hold a board out in the wind lengthwise and in just a few moments it would be sandpapered to a fine surface.[28]

Ray Harpham told me,

> We used to have an outhouse (backhouse we called it) firmly braced to be sure the wind during the year and the kids at Halloween didn't upset it. A tornado came along and it was solid enough to stay put but it turned it wrong side out. First we figured it wasn't hurt but investigation showed us the door and the seat were both on the same side. We couldn't use it that way but a lot of people came to see it. It was known far and wide as the inside outside outhouse.

In *Short Grass Country*[29] Stanley Vestal provides some of the classic stories that were told—certainly half in despair— about the heat, dust, and drought that all too frequently plagued the Plains. He tells how in Oklahoma dust was found to have penetrated into the impenetrable vault of a local bank, while the newspaper editor found the slat crate he used for a wastebasket filled to overflowing with dust. Perhaps it was the same editor who reported that gold nuggets blown up from the New Mexico mines had been found scattered about the town's streets.

It was easy to laugh at stories about spotting approaching duststorms—"Oklahoma rain" or "Kansas snow" as it was called—by listening for the rattlesnakes' sneezes or the persistent tale about the man who caught some bullfrogs and put them in his horsetank, only to have them drown because they had never learned how to swim. But it must have been with considerable pain and only an ironic smile that failing farmers said that they had been told by the county agent that they would no longer have to rotate their crops, because the Plains winds were rotating the soil, or that Texas and Oklahoma farmers would have to pay their taxes in Kansas now because that was where their farms had blown, or that some farmers who were not able to travel north with their farms would have to wait to plow them until they blew back down with the next change in the wind.

But if some farmers and journalists lied about the nature of such things, others were dogged guardians of the truth:[30]

> Some newspaper men are terrible liars. In writing of a cyclone out west one of them said it turned a well inside out, a cellar upside down, moved a township line, blew all the staves out of a whiskey barrel and left the bunghole, changed the day of the week, blew all the hair off a bald-headed man, blew a mortgage off a farm, blew all the cracks out of a fence, and knocked the wind out of a Populist.

Now doesn't that just bristle with righteous indignation? One has to wonder why the editor bothered to repeat each and every lie, if he was indeed so offended by them.

Tornados, as anyone will have to admit, are a very special breed of wind, and Plains folklore is shot through with the amazing exploits of these devious, mischievous whirlwinds:[31]

> The late tornado in Minnesota kicked up some queer pranks. It blew eight oxen over a river 800 yards wide. It took all the water out of a pond, carried it a mile and then set it down on Mayor Doran's farm in the shape of a small lake. It blew a man's boots off. Another man's coat was not only blown short, but actually buttoned from the top to the bottom. One old lady went up like a balloon, was carried two and a half miles, and was finally

landed astride a telegraph wire, where she was found by her grandson and relieved by a ladder. Judge Morgan says the wind not only carried off his dwelling house but his sub-cellar and two wells.

It appears that some folks would have made more of tornados than they actually were but I suppose it is merely a case of playing the shots as they lie, so to speak:[32]

The Omaha tornado, which swept through the city Easter Sunday on March 23, 1913, besides being out of place on the calendar, almost proved to be a wrecker of manmade reputations as well as buildings. . . . It seems that a substantial citizen and head of a family on that fateful day took a nap on the living room couch, and was still so engaged when the storm struck.

His recollection of the succeeding events is a trifle hazy and obscure but he does recall and sticks to it that he was fully clothed in his own conventional garb when he went to sleep.

But when he woke up he found himself in a strange home half a mile away from his own demolished residence and clothed only in a beribboned and lacy suit of lady's underwear.

His explanation of his predicament was readily excepted [sic] during the excitment of the moment, but later some folks including part of the immediate family became a trifle skeptical and it was necessary for friends to reassure them that tornados are inclined to be that way, even to the point of playfulness and practical joking. . . .

3

CATFISH AT
THE PUMP

> The mewl is a larger burd than a guse or turkey. It
> has two legs to walk with, and two more to kick with,
> and it wears its wings on the side of its hed.
>
> Josh Billings

> Three years ago a guileless tenderfoot came into
> Wyoming, leading a single Texas steer and carrying a
> branding iron; now he is the opulent possessor of six
> hundred head of fine cattle—the ostensible progeny of
> that one steer.
>
> Bill Nye

> If they don't understand what a deed it is to fight a
> grizzly bear with your bare hands, throw in another grizzly
> bear.
>
> Jim Bridger

> You can change a fool,
> but a doggone mule,
> is a mule until he dies.
>
> Uncle Dave Macon

I am always uneasy when I hear or tell a story from or
about O'Neill, Nebraska, because its history sounds very
much like a tall tale to me. It is like footnoting an important contribution in a scholarly paper with a passage from
Bill Nye or Josh Billings.

During the 19th century several presumably serious
attempts were made by the American Irish to somehow
secure the freedom of all Ireland from English rule. One

such attempt, under the leadership of General John J. O'Neill, was an effort to move up through Nebraska and the Dakotas, invade Canada, capture it, and hold it for ransom—to be traded to England for Ireland. Anyone who enjoys tall tales has to admire the sheer audacity of a plan like that!

Unfortunately, our less appreciative government got wind of the plan, seized the arms stored in a Lincoln, Nebraska, home, and nipped the plot in the bud. As a result the "army" settled down where they were and the site has become O'Neill, where St. Patrick's Day is celebrated with special zeal and the standard joke is "Do you know what I would be if I weren't Irish? Ashamed! Ashamed!"

Which is all by way of an introduction to this first pioneer Plains tale about animals[1]—the horse, so important that theft of one did actually mean death for the thief in those years:

There will be no racing of horses with transplanted glands at the O'Neill race track. The racing committee has announced that in the future horses entered in the speed events will have to wear their own glands to avoid accidents and complaints from other horse owners. Owners caught switching glands will be penalized the same as those discovered "hopping" or "juicing" their horses.

The racing committee's new rule was promulgated because of the scandalous action of Sapolio, belonging to the Jack McKenna stables, in the Beaver Flats derby the afternoon of July 4. The race was a mile and a furlong and some of the best horses at the meeting were entered.

Sapolio is the horse which Doc Wilkinson nearly ruined last fall by giving him some bucking horse glands by mistake in attempting to improve his spirit. He attempted to rectify the error this spring by grafting onto the horse some jack rabbit glands from a racing rabbit, belonging to Charles Harding. Before moving to Beaver Flats Mr. Harding had used the rabbit in coursing events at Oakland, California, where it was trained to beat it across the racing field when the dogs got after it and to escape through a hole in the fence at the farther side.

Sapolio in several private trials seemed to have been improved wonderfully by the rabbit glands and accordingly was entered in the Beaver Flats derby.

He got away fine with the other entries when the barrier went up and made the first round of the half mile track without any trouble arising. But halfway around the second time the yipping of the jockeys excited the lap dog belonging to Mrs. Charley Laughing Horse, who was watching the race from the tent of her husband's Indian show and the dog ran barking after the racing horse.

The effect on Sapolio was electrical, changing his stride from the easy swing of the gallopers to the stiff-legged spring of the former owner of his glands, and he drew away in frightened flight from the closely grouped contenders and distanced the others, passing under the wire, the winner.

This was not enough, however, and he tore on around the track again until he discovered a hole in the back of the fence, through which he promptly sought refuge, badly skinning up his rider and losing his saddle in the attempt.

The racing committee awarded the event to Sapolio but refused to accede to the demand of the doctor and Mr. McKenna for the entire purse because the other horses had been distanced. As a compromise it was decided to give second and third money to charity and the new rule was formulated at the insistence of the other horsemen.

But there are horses, and horses, and horses of another color:[2]

A broncho is a horse. He has four legs, like a sawhorse, but is decidedly more skittish. The broncho is of gentle deportment and modest mien, but there isn't a real safe place about him. There is nothing mean about a broncho though; he is perfectly reasonable and acts on principle. All he asks is to be let alone, but he does ask this, and even insists on it. He is firm in this matter, and no kind of argument can shake his determination. There is a broncho that lives out some miles from this city. We know him right well.

One day a man roped him and tried to put a saddle on him. The broncho looked sadly at him, shook his head and begged the fellow as plain as could be to go away and not try to interfere with a broncho who was simply engaged in the pursuit of his own happiness; but the man came on with the saddle and continued to aggress. Then the broncho reached out with his right hind foot and expostulated with him so that he died.

When thoroughly aroused the broncho is quite fatal, and if you can get close enough to him to examine his cranial structure you will find a cavity just above the eye where the bump of remorse should be.

The broncho is what the cowboys call "high strung." If you want to know just how high he is strung, climb up onto his apex. We rode a broncho once. We didn't travel far, but the ride was mighty exhilarating while it lasted. We got on with great pomp and a derrick, but we didn't put on any unnecessary style when we went to get off. The beast evinced considerable surprise when we took up our location upon his dorsal fin. He seemed to think a moment, and then he gathered up his loins and delivered a volley of heels and hardware, straight out from the shoulder. The recoil was fearful.

We saw that our seat was going to be contested, and we began to make a motion to dismount, but the beast had got under way this time, so we breathed a silent hymn and tightened our grip. He now went off into a spasm of tall, stiff-legged bucks. He pitched us so high that every time we started down we would meet him coming up on another trip.

Finally he gave us one grand farewell boost and we clove the firmament and split up through the hushed ethereal until our toes ached from the lowness of the temperature, and we could distinctly hear the music of the spheres.

When we came down and fell in a little heap about 100 yards from the starting point, a kind Samaritan gathered up our remains in a cigar box and carried us to the hospital. As they looked pityingly at us, the attendant surgeons marveled as to the nature of our mishap. One said it was a cyclone, another said that it was a railroad smash-up, but we thought of the calico-hided pony that was grazing peacefully in the dewy meadow, and held our peace.

The man's mistake was obvious: he confused a broncho with a horse. Never confuse a broncho with a horse. That is like confusing a rattler with a garter snake or a woman with a lady, and just as fatal in most cases.

Young ladies and gentlemen who have never ridden a

horse, or who ride one only when and where they want to, like horses. Cowboys who were very lonely sometimes liked horses. Some horses like horses. But that about sums it up. I could tell you about horses, but it would seem a shame to have a generally friendly, humorous, family book like this one labeled "To be read by children below eighteen years of age with parental guidance only."

I have tried to find solid evidence of equine sagacity and gentility to balance the argument but the search has not been impressively productive. In a left-handed sort of way, the following passage seems to say nice things about horses:[3]

When Dr. Chidester got the first automobile in Western [Wisconsin] he was out on a call and met a farmer and his wife driving a team of horses. The doctor stopped and got out to lead the horses past the car. The farmer said, "No! No! Lead my wife past. I can manage the horses."

And perhaps the next item can also be interpreted as a positive statement for horses, even though it is offered by its cowboy narrator as an item of disparagement:[4]

". . . I did own an ol' hoss one time that was about the *dumbest* critter I ever did see. I'll tell yuh what that fool horse did one night when I drunk too much likker and passed out in town. He picked me up and slung me on his back and carried me twenty miles to the ranch. When he got me there, he pulled off my boots with his teeth and nosed me inta my bunk. Then he went to the kitchen, fixed up a pot of coffee, and brung me a cup all fixed up with cream and sugar. Then the next day I had a hangover, and he went out all by hisself and dug post holes all day so's the boss would let me sleep. When I woke up and found out what that fool horse had done, I cussed him fer two days without stoppin' and wished 'im off on a greener which was passin' by. It was good riddance too!"

"I'd say that was a pretty smart horse," observed a listener. "What in the world did you get rid of him for?"

"Smart, heck! Who ever heard of a real cowboy usin' cream and sugar in his coffee? No wonder I had such a turrible hangover!"

I believe that those tales should go a long way toward

establishing the nature of the reputation the horse has among those who know him best. I would be delighted to press the case in court but that would be like arresting watermelon thieves while politicians go free because the horse, for all his dedication to the cause, is an admirable paragon of virtue when his character is compared to that of the unregenerate, irredeemable nature of the mule. So cantankerous is this creature that he earned the undying admiration of teamsters, miners, and other ne'er-do-wells in every frontier community.

The explosive quality of the mule is such that the act of the explosion itself is rarely described by man, it being far too fast in the transaction for the human eye. The phenomenon occurred with some regularity in pioneer communities and would send mothers scurrying to cover their children's ears. One such occasion was described by Bill Nye in the Laramie *Daily Sentinel*:[5]

> Last evening a man who was riding a mule along Fourth Street noticed that the animal walked a little lame, so he alighted, and, resting the mule's gambrel on his shoulder, he took a long tin spectacle case out of his pocket, and, adjusting his glasses, proceeded to examine the animal's hoof with great care.

> We called round at the man's residence early this morning to see how he was getting along. The doctor wouldn't allow him to talk much, on account of his fractured jaw, but we learned from his broken conversation that just as he had discovered that a large assortment of Chinese fireworks and Roman candles had worked in under the frog of the mule's foot, he found himself over in the courthouse yard, picking pieces of spectacles out of his face. The doctor says that he thinks he can save the third and fourth joints of the neck but the man will always have to wear a cork head and false face. This is just as it should be, for men who persist in looking into the behindest foot of a mule should always wear cork heads. It is very appropriate that they should.

The distinctive personality of the mule demanded some special concern and treatment on the part of the alleged owner. For example, it was widely known that most preachers were incapable of driving mules because they didn't speak the same language, literally. Drives to reduce the application of profanity by muleskinners resulted in delayed schedules and deserting teamsters until the benighted colonels or capitalists once more let the drivers caress the mules' ears with the tones of love and terms of endearment to which the mules so enthusiastically responded.

A widespread tale told of the greenhorn who purchased a mule from an able mule trainer but came walking back to the animal yard an hour later, disgruntled and exhausted. It seemed the mule had balked and bawled along leisurely for a few miles and then refused to walk another step unless it was at his speed and in the direction of his choosing.

"Well, did you talk reason with him?" asked the trader.

"I explained the situation to him as clearly as I could," puffed the exasperated dude.

So the seller, seeing right off that there had been a misunderstanding, got into a wagon and took the young man back to where the mule was enjoying the scenery and considering the rewards of a virtuous life. The mule trader picked up a fence post from the bed of his wagon, took a vicious 360° swing, and broke the post across the mule's head, just above his eyebrows. The mule staggered to his knees and arose with his eyes slightly crossed.

The trader got up into the saddle and said, "Git up," whereupon the mule moved briskly ahead and responded to the reins in like manner, smoothly and promptly.

"First you have to get his attention," the trader explained.

A McCook, Nebraska, newspaper on February 19, 1898, printed a story about a less dramatic but apparently equally efficacious application of logic on a mule:[6]

"I was riding along a hilly road in eastern Nebraska," remarked a traveling salesman, "when I saw a mule running toward me with a singletree dangling at his heels. With great difficulty I succeeded in turning out of his way, and he continued to go down the hill at a lively pace.

"About a mile farther on I saw two frontwheels of a spring wagon and a short distance away the other wheels and a wagon box. I looked around to see if the driver had been hurt, but, finding no one, I drove on.

"In a few minutes I met a man walking down the road rather hastily. 'Stranger,' he queried, 'did ye see a mewl down thar?'

" 'Yes.'

" 'Did he hav a rag over 'is year?'

" 'I didn't see any.'

" 'Waal, it's all right. I reckon 'e'll stop when 'e gits flustered out an' I reckon 'e's cured.'

" 'What is he cured of?' I asked.

" 'Balkin'. Ye see I heerd that a grasshopper put in the year o' a hoss or mewl'd cure 'im from balkin'; so I tied a rag over the critter's year so it couldn't git out, catched a grasshopper, put 'im in, an', stranger, it's the bes' remedy I ever seed. The mewl didn't give me time to git in the wagon. I never did see a mewl so sprightly. I reckon the hopper's got out now, an' I'll go on an' catch the mewl.' "

In one of those inevitable and fascinating contradictions that characterize life, the mule combined more strength and determination than a horse with about twice the frustrating troublesomeness. I was once told that when the load was particularly heavy or the ground especially loose or slippery, the farmer inevitably turned to his mules, for they would pull at the top of their strength, virtually dropping to their knees to get every possible bit of power into the harness. On the other hand, the use of mules required substantially more alertness on the part of the driver. Charlie I. Scudder of Omaha told me that when the farm horses were hitched to a wagon the reins could be dropped and the horses would stand there quietly, waiting for the next signal. But they had one mule, he said, that would watch for the slightest chance to trot away from the work crew, pulling the wagon back to the barn, so that someone would have to walk all the way back to the house to fetch the animals and their load. Mr. Scudder told me that he was once working in the fields with the mules and dropped the reins. He happened to see the mule look around and spy the reins lying loose on the ground. Mr. Scudder, thinking fast, stepped on the reins. The mule, realizing that he had been outwitted— for the moment—promptly sat down on the wagon tongue, broke it, and set back the work for a full day. The mule knew precisely what he had done and probably took considerable pride in his ingenuity and received a Sunday School award from his barn-mates for special accomplishment.

Other animals were capable of inflicting considerable damage on bystanders if they were not accorded due respect, as Bill Nye outlined in his famous book, *Bill Nye and Boomerang*:[7]

> A stock owner went out the other day over the divide to see how his cattle were standing the rigorous weather, and found a large, fine steer in his last long sleep. The stockman had to roll him over to see the brand, and he has regretted his curiousity ever· since. He told me that the brand looked to him like a Roman candle making about 2000 revolutions per moment, and with 187 more prismatic colors than he thought were in existence. Sometimes a steer is not dead but in a cold, sleepy stupor which precedes death, and when stirred up a little and irritated because he cannot die without turning over and showing his brand, he musters his remaining strength and kicks the inquisitive stockman so high he can see and recognize the features of departed friends. That was the way it happened on this occasion. The stockman fell in the branches of a pine tree on Jack Creek, not dead but very thoughtful. . . .

Homemade veterinarians, it seems, were frequently visited by such strange fireworks displays, judging from the number of reports of this kind one finds in the newspapers of the day:[8]

> A funny thing happened near McCook a while ago. A farmer went into his barn after dark with a lantern and found that one of his cows was swelled to twice its natural size as a result of gas generated in its insides by alfalfa which had not been properly cured. He rushed to the house to get a knife to perform a surgical operation upon the animal, leaving the lantern in the barn. Before he got back there came a burst like the solemn booming of a cannon. And such a sight met his eyes when he opened

the barn door! The cow had exploded and she was plastered all over the inside of the barn: her horns were driven two inches deep into an oak post, her various bones had gone through the roof, and there wasn't a piece of her hide big enough for a doormat. It remains for scientists to explain this phenomenon. Suffice it to say that the cow isn't giving milk any more.

* * *

Four years ago Charles Pierson, of Pierson's ranch on the Ravenna-St. Michael Road, lost a silver watch. He hunted high and low for it but could not find it. One evening last week while pailing the family mild [sic] milk cow he had his ear affectionately placed against Bossy's flank when he thought he heard a faint ticking. He listened attentively and finally felt sure that the sounds proceeded from the internal economy of the cow. He looked the beast over carefully, thinking something must be wrong with her—thought she might be in the first stages of the dreaded cornstalk disease.

For the next two or three days Mr. Pierson watched the cow carefully, and frequently listened for the mysterious sound within, and they were always plainly to be heard. Finally an idea occurred to Mr. Pierson and he took the cow out behind the barn, tied her to a strong post and swatted her one between the large soulful eyes with an axe. Then he cut her open and in her stomach found the long lost watch. It was running right along and had lost only three minutes in four years. The passage of food in the cow's stomach had kept it wound and running.

Then it occurred to Mr. Pierson that four years ago when he lost the watch the cow was a young and carefree heifer wandering about the premises and she had probably mistaken the watch for a turnip and swallowed it, and it remained with her until the last, an ever-present reminder of the slow passage of time.

The application of the breeding science that has given us fine stock seen on today's pastures and ·range produced some peculiar, now lost, aberrant forms along the way:[9]

There is a story that comes from Nemaha County [Nebraska] which, if true, will revolutionize the saloon business. Near the town of Peru is a farmer who is a graduate of one of the most noted agricultural colleges of Germany. By a series of experiments he has discoverd that by feeding a cow on hops, malt, and corn she can be transformed into a small brewery and made to produce the best quality of lager beer. It is ready for use after being corked up in jugs for a day or two.

A story which enjoyed some currency on the Plains frontier told of a cow that gave so much milk that the farmer had to milk her into the well instead of a bucket. Modern listeners always wonder what happened to those wonderful breeds of animals of yore, and in this case there is an answer to the question. Although the farmer tried to breed a herd of these fabulous critters, he found that the cow was physically incapable of bearing young. And it must have been a hereditary factor, for the cow's mother had also been sterile.

Pigs were not normal grist for the tall-tale mill but one of the most widely told of all tall tales on the frontier did deal with a pig, and has a conclusion that I reckon among the champion snappers and thigh slappers of the whole genre:[10]

> A local farmer bought several cases of dynamite to shake loose some stumps that had been bothering him for some time. He set the boxes down on the porch while he went in for lunch, and along came his best sow and ate the whole of both boxes. The pig carelessly walked too close to the business end of the farm mule and when the mule let him have it, the dynamite exploded. Killed the mule, destroyed the barn and the house, and the hog was sick for a week.

Mitchell Pass in western Nebraska is a narrow gate between two towering buttes, through which a goodly number of the Oregon Trail travelers passed. Pigs are not a part of the ordinary livestock of that part of the country, but then neither is the news item from the Gering *Courier*, December 22, 1893, a run-of-the-mill news story:[11]

> John R. Stilts, the urbane, relates that a short time since he purchased a common ordinary hog—with no particular promise of ordinary growth. He took it over to his ranch to fatten it and it imbibed the rich nutriments

that run amuck in the Mitchell Valley, so that when he started to drive it over to market, Mr. Porker got stuck in the Pass and John had to back him out to wait until the river froze and he could skid him down on the ice.

Of all animals the dog has always been man's favorite and vice versa, I suppose. As in the case of the mule, even the most cantankerous ones managed to gain some praise in the hearts and tall tales of their human idolators.

Bill Nye was capable, so far as I can tell, of being caustic and unromantic about everything in this world, and at one time or another lambasted most of those things in print. Nowhere else did he wax quite so eloquent however, or conclude with such redolent praise, as he did in this essay from his *Bill Nye and Boomerang*, "The Duke of Rawhide":[12]

"I believe I've got about the most instinct bulldog in the United States," said Cayote Van Gobb yesterday. "Other pups may show cuteness and cunning, you know, but my dog, the Duke of Rawhide Buttes, is not only generally smart, but he keeps up with the times. He's not only a talented cuss, but his genius is always fresh and original."

"What are some of his specialties, Van?" said I.

"Oh, there's a good many of 'em, fust and last. He never seems to be content with the achievements that please other dogs. You watch him and you'll see that his mind is active all the time. When he is still he's working up some scheme or another, that he will ripen and fructify later on.

"For three years I've had a watermelon patch and run it with more or less success, I reckon. The Duke has tended to 'em after they got ripe, and I was going to say that it kept his hands pretty busy to do it, but, to be more accurate, I should say that it kept his mouth full. Hardly a night after the melons got ripe and in the dark of the moon, but the Duke would sample a cowboy or a sheepherder from the lower Poudre. Watermelons were generally worth ten cents a pound along the Union Pacific for the first two weeks, and a fifty-pounder was worth $5. That made it an object to keep your melons, for in a good year you could grow enough on ten acres to pay off the national debt.

"Well, to return to my subject, Duke would sleep days during the season and gather fragments of the rear breadths of Western pantaloons at night. One morning Duke had a piece of fancy cassimere in his teeth that I tried to pry out and preserve, so that I could identify the owner, perhaps, but he wouldn't give it up. I coaxed him and lammed him across the face and eyes with an old board, but he wouldn't give it to me. Then I watched him. I've been watchin' him ever since. He took all these fragments of goods, I found, over into the garret above the carriage shed.

"Yesterday I went in there and took a lantern with me. There on the floor the Duke of Rawhide had arranged all the samples of Rocky Mountain pantaloons with a good deal of taste, and I don't suppose you'd believe it, but that blamed pup is collecting all these little scraps to make himself a crazy quilt.

"You can talk about instinct in animals, but, so far as the Duke of Rawhide Buttes is concerned, it seems to me more like all-wool genius a yard wide."

On the other hand, pity the poor soul who might have tried to lie to Bill Nye about the canine world, because, from the evidence disclosed in Nye's story, "The Gentle Youth from Leadville," also from *Bill Nye and Boomerang*, the would-be prevaricator would probably find himself yearning for the tender mercies of the Spanish Inquisition:[13]

In addition to the other attractions about the depot, the old museum of curiousities from the Rocky Mountains has been re-opened. I like to go down and listen to the remarks of overland passengers relative to these articles. There are two stuffed coyotes chained to the door, one on each side, and it amuses me to see a solicitous parent nearly yank his little son to pieces for going so near these ferocious animals. The coyotes look very lifelike and show their teeth a good deal, but it breaks a man all up when he finds that their digestive apparatus has been replaced with sawdust and plaster of Paris.

After a coyote gets to padding himself out with baled hay and cotton so as to look plump, he loses his elasticity of spirits, and we cease to respect him. Sometimes a tourist asks if these coyotes are prairie dogs.

A few days ago a man from Michigan, who has been here two weeks and wears a large buckskin patch where it will do the most good, and who is very bitter in his remarks about "tenderfeet," was standing at the depot, when a young man, evidently from a theological seminary, came along from the train whistling, "What a friend we have in Jesus." He walked up to the Michigan man, who began to look fierce, and timidly asked if he would tell him all about the coyote. The Michigan man, who never had seen a live coyote in his life, volunteered to tell him some of the finest decorated lies, with venetian blinds and other trimmings to them, while the young man stood there in open-mouthed wonder, with daylight visible between his legs as high as the fifth rib. I never saw such a picture of rapt attention in my life. As he became more interested, the Michigan man warmed up to his work and lied to this guileless youth till the perspiration rolled down his face. As the train started out, the delegate to the Young Men's Christian Association asked the Michigan man for his address. "I want the address of some good earnest liar," he said, "one who can lie by the day, or by the job, and endure the strain. I want a man to enter the field for the championship of America. Any communication you may wish to make will reach me at Leadville, Colorado. I have been in the Rocky Mountains ever since I was three years old, and have lived for weeks on no other diet but coyote on toast and raw Michigan man." He waved his hand at the M. man, and said, "If I don't see you again, hello!" and he was gone. How many such little episodes we experience on our journey to the tomb.

The first page of the first issue of the Grand Island *Independent* must have been a trifle short of international news or items about volcanos or tidal waves in Nebraska because a good part of one full column was devoted to this tale of journalistic trial and tribulation:[14]

A communication from our reporter in North Platte:
Deer Boss.
You axed me tu send yew a full report if enny thing verry startlin occurd which it did as follers, viz: namely, to-whit:
I was a standin over bi mister Dicks drug stoer a wile ago, when I hearn the gaul darndest racket i ever hearn since june the 11 when them fellers war arter us. I looked down the street and thair i seed the biggest kind ov an

ister can with a hundred pound dorg tied to its tale jist a hopin it up toward joolsburg. Sumtimes the purp was a hed and sumtimes the can. it war the titest race i ever seed an drawd a bigger crowd than the duch preecher did. The majors coly dorg tuk arter the otfit & awa they awl went for the west. I hearn one kuss with his shurt collar open, and a white muslin cap on remark "purty work," tho what those air i dont no. old coly just stretched his self out & got rite down tu squar runnin like his nex months beaf stake depended on ketchin that ister kan, which wuz gitten awa with that unfortunity purp faster ner big John C. kan git awa with Durr's straw-bery pize. Iff that kan kept on at the gate it was going when i last seed it, it must have dropt a sum place up the road.

This is the only item of importance ive bin abel tu steel this weak. will tri & raik up sumthin better nex weak.

Until then adoo. Yoors till deth,
Loyle Reporter.

Pee Ess. We hav jist received a reply. from Shian statin that a ister kan with a dorg's tale & hine laigs hangin tu it had jist passed like a stroke of litenin—ole coly cum in about a mile and a haf behind, almost gin out. He guv up the chase thar, and will start hum in the mornin, a sadder and a wiser dorg.

A story that was told wherever and whenever dog lovers met, from the East Coast right up to the frontier, dealt with the brave dog that persisted in barking and pulling at his master's bed covers one night even though the sleepy man furiously pounded on the dog's noggin with a rolled newspaper. Finally the dog succeeded in getting the man up, down the stairs, and out the front door, at which point the now grateful master realized that the house had been on fire. Not satisfied with one heroic deed, the dog rushed back into the blazing house to rescue the man's wife, and then three more times to drag the sleepy children to safety.

The man was prepared to welcome the dog to a life of eternal comfort and ease—when the dog turned again and ran back into the flaming house. Now the man *was* mystified, for all members of the family were safely out of the house.

Imagine the man's joy and relief however when he saw

the dog come tearing out of the house carrying the fire insurance policy that he had retrieved from the top left desk drawer in the study.[15]

The prairie dog is not really a member of the canine family at all but was a sort of tall tale in the flesh:[16]

The prairie dog exemplified what frequently happened when men crossed the line [of the frontier into the Plains]. In the East men were accustomed to a squirrel that climbed trees; when they struck the Plains they found that the animal no longer went up but down. The contrast was more than their minds could grasp, and so they made the Plains squirrel a dog!

Lowell Thomas received a story about a dog so smart that when night hunting he would catch a toad, feed him with lightning bugs until he glowed like a lantern, and then carry him around to light his way to the game.[17]

Stories abound about the strange consequences resulting from chickens eating varied and peculiar things. They eat sawdust and lay boards, eat fireflies and lay lightbulbs, or eat nails and lay hand grenades. Without question, the most depressing chicken story I have ever encountered is this gem, incorporating greed, loyalty, determination, and tragedy—all the elements of great drama:[18]

The *Springfield Republican*, in speaking of a new invention for a hen's nest, whereby the eggs drop through a trapdoor, and so deceive the hen that she keeps on laying, is responsible for the following:

"Blobbs met with a loss however with one of the persuaders. Blobbs had a lovely young Shanghai pullet, of boundless ambition. Blobbs bought her a persuader, and his lovely Shanghai used it. She went upon the nest in the morning. Blobbs saw her go, and his heart bounded within him. Alas! he never saw her come off again. At night he visited the persuader. In the upper compartment was a handful of feathers, a few toe-nails, and a bill. In the lower compartment were three dozen eggs. Blobbs saw it all. Her delicate constitution had been unequal to the effort, and, fired by young ambition, she had layed herself all away."

Chickens are rarely thought of today as being barnyard intellectuals but there is some evidence that pioneer chickens were at least capable of learning a few survival tricks:[19]

A man out West says that he moved so often during one year that whenever a covered wagon stopped at his gate his chickens would fall on their backs and hold up their feet, in order to be tied and thrown in.

Animals like the prairie dog and rattlesnake were new to the homesteaders and couldn't have been conjured up in their worst dreams, and there were other creatures too, also subjects for the tall-tale master's creative talents:[20]

A traveling man in White Sulphur Springs makes a bet of drinks in the town with Coates, the saloonkeeper, that Coates can't find a man who will hold up his hand and take his oath that he has seen 100,000 buffalo at one sight. When the bet's decided, it's agreed to ring the triangle at the hotel, which will call the town to their drinks.

Many old-timers said they had seen that many buffalo, but refused to swear to it, and it looked like Coates would lose his bet until Milt Crowthers showed up. Then a smile of confidence spread over Coates' face as he introduced Crowthers to the drummer.

"Mr. Crowthers," said the traveling man, "how many antelope have you seen at one time?"

Crowthers straightens up and looks wise, like he's turning back over the pages of the past, "Two hundred thousand," says he.

"How many elk?" asks the traveling man.

"Somethin' over a million," replies Crowthers.

"Mr. Crowthers, how many buffalo will you hold up your hand and swear you have seen at one sight?"

Crowthers holds up his hand. "As near as I can figure," says he, "about three million billion."

This is where Coates starts for the triangle, but the traveling man halts him, saying, "Where were you when you saw these buffalo, Mr. Crowthers?"

"I was a boy travelin' with a wagon train," replies Crowthers. "We was south of the Platte when we was forced to corral our wagons to keep our stock from bein' stampeded by buffalo. For five days an' nights 50 men kep' their guns hot killin' buffalo. The sixth day the herd spread, givin' us time to yoke up an' cross the Platte an' it's a damn good thing we did."

"Why?" asks the traveling man.

"Well," says Crowthers, "We no more than hit the high country north of the Platte, than lookin' back, here comes the main herd!"

There were many new animals for migrants to the frontier, and most were adapted to easy use in the tall tale, but no animal attained the ranks of exaggeration and wonder that was reserved for the jackass rabbit—"jack" for short. His enormous ears, irrepressible reproductivity, and dazzling speed made him the subject of many a conversation around potbelly stoves:[21]

"Talking about lightning," said a passenger from the West, "if you want to see lightning that's lightning just go out into western Nebraska. That's where it lightnings for all that's out. But I'll never forget how I was fooled out there one day. A few days after I got there I was going across the prairie with a friend of mine when I saw something that caused my hair to stand on end. It was a streak of lightning going across the prairie in leaps, as if it were an animal. My eye could hardly follow it, it went so fast. "Well," says I to my friend, "that beats all the lightning I ever heard tell of. I've seen forked lightning, and sheet lightning, but I never seen lightning follow the ground like that."

"That's where you're off," says my friend. "That hain't lightning at all—it's a jack rabbit out exercising hisself."

Tall tales can be very troublesome when it comes to hunting. Boasting has its limits and its disastrous results. There is, for instance, the story about the hunter who comes out of the field and stops in a small-town saloon where he proceeds to regale one of the men at the bar with stories of his hunting prowess and the day's successes. "Downed nearly thirty ducks to start the morning, three of them with a single shot."

The listener seemed unimpressed.

"Bagged four deer, two bucks and two doe, in that woods just off the road."

No comment from the audience.

"Quit hunting at noon, threw a line in Johnson's Creek and pulled out nearly eighty trout by suppertime."

Still the other drinker said nothing.

"Why don't you say something?" asked the mighty hunter.

"Do you know who I am?" asked the listener.

"No."

"I'm the new game warden for this area."

There was a moment's silence, and then the hunter asked, "Do you know who I am?"

"No."

"Well, I'm the new champion liar for this area."

On the other end of the scale, I have always admired the observation of the young John Neihardt, who found himself and his companions short on food while on a float down the Missouri River during the early part of the century. They ·spotted quite a number of deer tracks on the bank but, as Neihardt wrote,[22] ". . . It has long been conceded that the tracks are by far the least edible things pertaining to an animal."

Of all sportsmen the fisherman is the most interesting to the folklorist because so much of what he says is unvarnished folklore. Folk poesie provides an ancient and eternally accurate description of the fisherman's art and craft:[23]

> Behold the fisherman!
> He riseth early in the morning and disturbeth the whole household.
> Mighty are his prospects.
> He goeth forth full of hope and when the day is far spent he returneth smelling of strong drink; and the truth is not in him.

"And the truth is not in him," indeed! Of all fishermen's tall tales that are indeed tales, that is which have the redeeming quality of at least a hint of narrative rather than being unabashed and unadulterated falsehood, the following is one of the most widely distributed and recounted:[24]

> An early settler was fishing and ran out of bait. He looked around for a frog or something suitable, but couldn't find a thing. Until he ran across a little garter snake crawling along with a frog in its mouth, headed home with supper, I guess. Well, the fisherman caught the snake and took the frog away from him. He put it on the hook and tossed his line out into the water and settled back for a nice afternoon's fishing.

Later he happened to glance over at the snake and found him just lying there, obviously brokenhearted at the loss of the frog. So the kindhearted fisherman picked up the snake and poured a little of his whiskey down the snake's throat, as a sort of pick-me-up. The snake wiggled off, clearly feeling much better, and the fisherman went back to *his* work.

About fifteen minutes later the fisherman felt something rubbing up against his ankle and he looked down to find the little snake with another frog in its mouth.

A similar story[25] dealt with a man who had some whiskey but had also carried along enough bait for the day. The fish were not biting, so by way of experimentation the fisherman dipped a good-sized worm in the whiskey and then put him on the line. After only a couple of seconds there was a tremendous strike on the line and a terrible battle ensued. The fisherman was certain that he had discovered a real secret: fish like the taste of whiskey. But when he pulled the line up he found that the worm had actually sought out a grandaddy bass in his hole, beat the tar out of him, and was bringing him back under his arm [!] to the fisherman.

Lowell Thomas in his collection of tall tales[26] had some sworn testimony of places where fish were so big that live tomcats were used as bait, or where fishermen were so sneaky that they would toss a few "plugs" of chewing tobacco into the water and then belt the lunkers over the head with an oar when they came up to spit.

On the Plains, I must remind you, such stories have to be taken one at a time, with a grain of salt, but sometimes as the Gospel truth. In July of 1971, for example, a Nebraska farmer complained,[27] "I've lost beets to hail, freeze, nematode, and mud, but this is the first year they've ever been eaten off by carp." It seems that during a wet spring the carp had come up the irrigation ditches from the river and into the field rows where they rooted the young plants right out of the ground and ate them. I have often wondered if the farmer in question ever got that claim—or any subsequent ones—past the insurance adjustor.

So, in light of that complaint, which is presumably

totally honest, how was the 19th-century reader supposed to doubt the authenticity of the following item, from the files of a Police Judge, no less:[28]

> Police Judge Holmes went fishing Saturday. He came home with a catfish weighing 25 pounds under his arm. The judge said the catfish had been found guilty of assault and battery and was to be sentenced to solitary confinement. The judge was walking along the banks of the Platte, and suddenly the catfish came out and chased him about half a mile. The judge had no weapon but suddenly seized a piece of board and smashed the fish over the head.

Indeed, it becomes obvious upon examining a few more newspaper records that the catfish of the pioneer years matched the homesteaders when it came to tenacity and unconventional boldness:[29]

> A catfish weighing 67 pounds was on exhibition in Boggs and Baldruff's shop yesterday. It was caught in the Platte River. It seems that it had gone up into the grass early in the morning to get a drink of dew and was killed with a club before it could get back to its native sand bed.

And from another source:[30]

> The life of a farmer on the bottom lands in the eastern part of the county is full of trials these wet days. Commissioner Berry (and his neighbors are, no doubt, in the same fix) is worried half to death by the catfish jumping into his hog pen and snapping at the porkers' heels.

It would be easy enough to scoff at such items if clear proof, like that closing this article from the Fremont [Nebraska] *Daily Herald* of August 8, 1894, were not freely and openly provided:[31]

> A party of youngsters who were camping and fishing on the Elkhorn had a novel experience the other evening. They were getting water out of a pump when they were attacked by four immense catfish who were apparently desperate for a drink of water. After a lively battle they managed to lasso three of the fish, while the other got away. The boys brought the captives to the city and sold them for two dollars. Anybody who doubts this fish story can go out to Elkhorn and see the pump.

There was a time when landlubbers believed that any

crew that could bring a ship to tack upwind must assuredly be in league with the devil, and then it came to be the Sunday-sailor's mildest challenge. There was a time when Yellowstone Park geography was believed to be a symptom of too much time alone in the woods for John Colter and Jim Bridger. There was a time when someone might have thought it a joke that catfish would come up on the land and challenge whatever it encountered—until the walking catfish of Florida began strolling about from pool to pool, eating dog food out of bowls, and intimidating the rightful canine claimants. So it is then with this next story; do not be too confident in your skepticism:[32]

> An angler hooked a perch one morning while fishing in the Platte. He played the fish all day, but was unable to land it. He moored it to the bank with his line and went home to rest. After a good night's sleep he returned to his task, but still was unable to land the monster.
>
> Days went by in this routine, and finally he hauled it ashore. He dragged it home but its weight was so great he sank to his knees on the pavement at every step as he tugged at his prize.
>
> The fish was so large he was unable to kill it. He kept it alive in a huge tank he had constructed and removed fillets from its flanks as needed for the table. Eventually, he moved back East and, on leaving, gave the fish to a widow. She wrote him from time to time, in ensuing years, saying she had gradually sliced in to where "the fillets are getting right good." She told the angler the perch often asked about him.

Lies about fish have usually stemmed from the overly proud or presumptive fisherman, and therefore the size and ferocity have been points of real affection. Snakes too have always been a fascination. But less positive in nature. We are not so much frightened by them, it seems to me, as we are fascinated by them, like trembling sparrows waiting for the strike. Their motion, the scales—wet yet dry, the piercing eyes and probing tongue, the Biblical curse, captivate us. Everyone has a snake story. Jesse Hill Ford capitalized on that factor in his short story, "The Surest Thing in Show Business,"[33] a story about snakes and people:

. . . I've learned one thing after twenty-five years in show business: it's the fact that there ain't a single living American that ain't had a great-grandaddy or a step-uncle or some connection like that who was swallered whole by a rattler. Understand, they never *knew* him, but Granny told them about it, which makes the rattlesnake the surest money-maker in American show business. They will pay to see what swallered Grandaddy every time.

Or maybe they will just make up another story about the event![34]

That brings to mind . . . ol' Peg-Leg Dooley, who onc't had a rattlesnake for a pet. Now, you gents may figger I'm tryin' to string up a bunch o' nonsense, but I'll explain 'zactly how it happened. An', by the way, how ol' Pete got that peg leg.

It seems ol' Pete was up in Oklahoma Territory one fall an' had to make camp in that shinnery [sic] country. Wal, he had heard how that country was full o' rattlesnakes, so he figgered he'd tie a hammock up between two shinnery [sic] trees when he bedded down. It was pretty dark by that time an' it was only after considerable gropin' 'round that Pete got his hammock tied up. Durin' the night he felt that hammock swingin' quite a bit, but he blamed it on the Oklahoma wind. But the next morning when he woke up, derned if he didn't find that he had tied that hammock up with a pair of live rattlers!

Wal, ol' Pete was pretty skitterish after that an' packed up as quick as he could an' started to kite outa there. But about that time his hoss stepped in a gopher hole an' pinned him to the ground. Pete was in a turrible fix an' thought he was doomed to die right there, but he got an idea that saved his life. He walked to the nearest ranch an' borrowed an axe. Then he came back and chopped off his leg and set hisself free.

Then, after Pete had cut him a peg leg outa a shin-oak tree, he skedaddled for home. When he got there, he found a baby rattlesnake, which had struck him on the peg leg an' hadn't been able to get loose. It was a cute lil' critter, an' Pete decided to keep him for sort of a combination pet an' souveynir of his visit to Oklahomy.

After that, Pete became real attached to that rattlesnake, which he named Elmer, an' Elmer to him. In fact, Elmer got so he was a regular watchdog an' guarded

Pete's shack. One night, while Pete was gone, a thief busted into the shack, an' Elmer was on the job. He captured that ol' robber by wrappin' hisself around one o' the feller's legs an' a leg o' the table. Then he stuck his tail through the keyhole o' the door an' rattled until the law came.

By and by Elmer grew up into one o' the biggest rattlesnakes anybody had ever seen. He wasn't so long, but he was about a foot thick. It got so he was the talk o' the whole country, an' ol' P. T. Barnum came down an' offered to buy him off Pete. But Pete was plum sentimental about that snake, like I said, an' wouldn't let him go. But he got to thinkin' that he couldn't stand in the way o' fame an' fortune fer Elmer, an' agreed to loan him out to the circus.

They stuck Elmer in a box an' hied him off in the baggage car of a train. Well, after a while Elmer got lonesome an' chewed his way outa the box. About that time the train started up a steep grade an' the couplin' busted. So what do you think ol' Elmer did? Why, he wrapped his head 'round one brake wheel and his tail 'round the other an' held the train together until they reached the next station! But all that strain on Elmer stretched him out until he was about thirty feet long. The circus had to advertize him as a boa constrictor instead of a rattlesnake.

In the fall of 1970 there was a flurry of letters sent to the "Public Pulse" column of the *Omaha World-Herald* debating the nature and disposition of the famed hoop snake.[35] Hoop snakes were notorious for grabbing their tails in their mouths and going off rolling at great speeds across the prairie grass. They bore a horn on their tail and if they struck with it, look out! It could kill a man instantly and it could swell a hoe handle up to the size of a telephone pole. The first of the "Public Pulse" letters seemed innocent enough:

On August 9 at 4:30 p.m. while returning from Plattsmouth I saw a hoop snake rolling on the sand on the east side of the Platte River Bridge. I stopped on the bridge to watch it and a car went around me, blowing his horn.

Evidently the noise scared the snake, for it unhooped itself and slithered into the river. The hoop appeared to be about three feet high, which would make the snake about 10 feet long.

(Signed) Commoner

But the letters written in response to this one got wilder and wilder:

I thought hoop snakes were long gone, although when I was a lad herding cows on the prairie I saw lots of them. After breakfast I'd go out to the end of the path and wise up on what women wore under their Mother Hubbards from the Sears catalogue, then rip out a couple of pages to put in my pocket and head the cows to the grass.

While they were grazing, I'd scout around for some Indian tobacco, pick a few leaves and strip a few from a snakeroot bush. I'd shred these up and lay the mixture to dry.

When the cows lay down to chew their cuds, I'd tear out a corset or such from the pages I'd brought and roll me a king-sized cig, light her up, and lie back in the grass.

Seems the smoke roused all the snakes in the territory, and they'd come around and hooper up. They'd go rollin' and twirlin' faster and faster, and the sun shining on their bright skins was a dazzler. Trouble was, all snakes' teeth slant backwards. Once they grab onto anything, it's a one-way street. The hoops got smaller and smaller, below doughnut size, and then, phtt! Ends met, end snakes, and story. Sorry kids, no orders filled.

(signed) Irvin Hogg

And yet another sample of the kind of response that original letter brought forth:

All these snake letters remind me of my Grandfather Reed, who was a muleskinner around the turn of the century on the plains of Nebraska and Kansas. When sleeping on the ground he always laid a rope in a circle and slept within the loop. Everyone knew that a rattlesnake wouldn't crawl over a rope. He woke one night to the sound of rattles, only to find two snakes holding up the rope while a third crawled underneath.

(signed) Dixie Lee Tripp.

Although the evil, bad reputations of the hoop snakes and rattlers tended to besmirch and slander the character of all reptiles, there was some evidence offered to the contrary:[36]

A valued subscriber of the *Journal* relates a most touching story of the devotion and unselfishness of a pet snake which sacrificed its own life to save the property of its master. The snake was 14 feet long, and was given to the gentleman by his father, who charged him to take care of it as though it were a child. Having a loving disposition, the snake soon became a household pet, and all sorts of caresses were lavished upon it. The other night a storm occurred, and the lightning was terrific. Several buildings in the neighborhood were struck and destroyed, and the snake, seeing the havoc, determined that it would save its benefactor's house. It took the tine of a pitchfork in its mouth, crawled up to the roof and stood on end with the tine pointing upwards, acting as a lightning rod for hours, when the electric current struck it and it fell to the earth a corpse.

Of all insects, it was the grasshopper that most captured the imagination and hate of the sodbuster. And why not? Imagine the horror of seeing a fierce black storm sweeping in from the West; as it approaches, the sound it makes is ominously unfamiliar. Then the first few gusts blow across the farmyard, and it becomes painfully evident that it is not a rainstorm or duststorm at all, but a 'hopper storm. Of course the crawling, gnawing pests were infinitely more destructive than rain, hail, snow, or dust but beyond that they were also more disgusting.

They ate the soft parts of fence posts and hoe handles and made them useless. They transformed the laundry drying on the line into lacy tatters. They destroyed valuable horse harness, leaving only the hardware in a pile on the floor next to the wall. They ate the tops off the turnips and onions and carrots in the garden—and then ate the roots right down into the ground, leaving nothing for the sobbing housewife who had been planning to feed her family through the winter with that garden. She now had only a mocking hole in the ground, a mold of the desperately needed vegetables. And of course the field crops were gone too, disappeared in a matter of hours or days.

Could the settlers laugh at the misery of a situation like that? Of course they could, and they did:[37]

There are lots of people who remember the summer, fall and winter of 1874; hot winds, grasshoppers, and government aid. First, came the hot winds. They were like a furnace, and would blister the hands and face like fire. We had to get into the house and shut the windows and doors to keep cool. A few days later came the grasshoppers, and they were a hungry bunch of tramps. They got everything that was green, and ate a good many things that were not green. They ate up forty rods of stone fence in thirty-seven and a half minutes by the watch. They destroyed more stone fences that fall than all the boys, dogs, and rabbits put together. The green-headed horseflies were pretty bad that fall, and they made it hot for the stock. We had a´ pet cow, and in order to keep the flies from eating her, we covered her with some green paint that we had left over after painting the house. The hoppers came along, ate up the cow, paint and all.

The hoppers would hold up the children on their way to school and take their lunches away from them. After the grasshoppers had eaten everything, we turned in and ate the grasshoppers. One old fellow said he used to live with the Digger Indians in Idaho, and they considered a grasshopper equal to or better than oysters, crawdads, clams, chili, or chop suey. So we all learned to eat grasshoppers, and I can say from experience that they were fine; but I do not want to live long enough to eat them three times a day again. After that we had grasshoppers for about six weeks and had them cooked and served in every way that could be thought of.

Now, just as I cautioned in the case of snakes, do not let the grasshopper horror sour you on all of the insect world. There *were* others that deserved the contempt, of course—fleas and "graybacks"—that found the porous walls of the sod house and the chinks in the log house the perfect place to raise a family:[38]

He called himself a "commercial traveler" but the vulgar people styled him a "drummer." He walked into a hotel office and proceeded to place his several pieces of luggage in the keeping of a son of Ham. Then he carelessly took up a pen and was registering his name when a good-sized sample of the *cimex lectularius* made its way slowly across the page of the register. The drummer stopped suddenly, and, after taking a long look at the insect, he cried, "Well, I've traveled all over the United States, and put up at all sorts of hotels, but I'm blessed if this isn't the first house I ever struck where these things come downstairs and find out the number of a fellow's room!"

It is true, I believe, that there were far more fleas, bed-bugs, and lice on the frontier than we enjoy today, but certainly a part of the problem lay in the elusive nature of the beast and some mitigating circumstances. For instance, I was told that one hotelkeeper would always answer the query, "Do your beds have bedbugs?" with "Not a single one," on the theory that virtually all bedbugs are married and have children.[39] A man who ought to know[40] told me that cow-pokes in eastern Wyoming made a habit of throwing a couple of snapping turtles—which are capable of taking a man's hand off in a single snarling crunch!—into a greenhorn's sleeping bag and then explaining to him that they were fairly ordinary western bedbugs.

Even fleas, lice, and other insects could however become friends of man out on the Plains frontier where there were so few men to be the friends of man. This next tale elevates the humble bug—and how harsh a term that seems to be in this context!—to the hallowed esteem usually reserved for dogs, good rifles, and bartenders:[41]

My neighbor Tom Brown come in just as I was finishing up my breakfast of hot biscuits and honey. Tom was helping us build fence over on the south forty and it just happened that every morning when he came to ride over the fence with us that I was eating biscuits and honey. So Tom wanted to know how come I had hot biscuits and honey every morning so I told him how it happened.

We once had several hives of bees. As there wasn't much fruit in that section of the country and transportation facilities were mostly lacking, there was a big demand for honey. For some reason or other the women folks in the neighborhood took a great notion for making hot biscuits and this increased honey sales. Everything was going fine till the bees took a notion to swarm. Sometimes a flock of bees would fly for miles trying to swarm and find a new home. Well, the bees would settle in some neighbor's corncrib or a scrub tree that had survived the wind and drouth. The neighbors were mostly honest and when they discovered the bees they would notify me when they saw me, and I would go and get the swarm and bring them home.

One day I went to Ike Jones' to get a swarm of bees. Ike had a mean youngster about fourteen years old. Tying two cats together by the tails and throwing them over a clothesline to watch them fight was his idea of fun.

When I went into the house to ask where the swarm of bees was there sat that tarnashun kid at the table watching a bee limp away from him and laughing to beat anything. I asked him what he was doing and he said, "I'll teach that bee not to try to sting me." Then he showed me the bee's stinger laying there. He had held the bee and cut off its stinger. The bee had kicked so hard while the boy was cutting off his stinger that he hurt his leg. While we were talking the boy gave the bee a push with a tooth-pick and the bee fell down. He couldn't walk any more. I got pretty mad, especially when I see that was my pet bee, Pheneas. I picked him up and he fainted away right there in my hand. I examined his leg and found that he had a fractured tibia. I commenced to cuss that ornery kid and when I was just going good his father came in and said, "Say, how do you know that's your bee, anyway?"

Well, that did make me mad, to think I didn't even know my favorite bee and besides we'd just got through marking them on the left hip with my initials in red paint. Well, I just pointed to my initials on Pheneas' hip and Ike had nothing to say. I wrapped Pheneas up in my handkerchief, put him in my pocket, went out, and drove the rest of those bees home.

When I got home I found that besides having a broken leg, Pheneas' knee cap was out of place. I doctored him and in about three weeks he was as good as new.

Pheneas was so grateful that ever since then, every morning, he comes buzzing in just as the hot biscuits are coming out of the oven and deposits a hunk of honey on my plate about as big as a walnut.

And like the dog, the insect is capable of being much more than interesting, much more than a friend—actually helpful and useful for mankind:[42]

A friend in California writes us that they have fire-flies so large in that State that they use them to cook by. They hang the kettles on their hind legs, which are bent for the purpose like pothooks.

The Plains are usually not thought of in terms of bears, but it is a historical fact that the wooded creeks and rivers were frequented by all manner of bear. They were driven out well in advance of the frontier but there are some stories that remind us of the days when the bruin were a present danger. The following report is above question because it was sent to me in a letter by Ray Harpham of Holstein, Nebraska, a witness beyond reproach:

The new preacher had been in his first church for a few weeks and wasn't such a much. After about six weeks he thought he had a very good sermon lined up. When he got to church however he discovered he was the only one there. Not wishing to waste his sermon he went ahead and delivered it. After the sermon he passed the collection plate and put in his collar button. That made the collection as good as last week's. Then he made a motion to double his salary. No one voted against it so that carried. He then hurried home to tell his wife about the raise.

She gave him some static about putting his collar button in the plate and went home to mama. Feeling a bit depressed he went out and sat down on a log. A bear came along and ate him up.

Two days later his wife relented and came back but when she found out he had a new bearskin coat while she was wearing last year's rag, she left for mama's again.

The bear told me all about it. My mother was scared by a bear before I was born and I was born bare, so I used to chat with bears all the time and that's the bear facts of the preacher and the bear.

Even after the bears had left the land to the settlers there were creatures to be dealt with. There was, for example, the dreaded Nebraska porcupine, seen only in the fall (a dog covered with cockleburs!).[43] And rats in Nebraska corncribs were reported to be so big that cats would walk about at night only in pairs.

When all was said and done, however, the strangest

creature of all, the one that excited the most wonder and admiration was the new frontiersman, the fresh migrant, the greenhorn, the greener. Word of a newcomer in camp or community would bring sparkly-eyed jokers from miles around, anxious to plumb the depth s of the innocent's gullibility:[44]

A newcomer to the Plains was asking what the homesteaders could possibly find to eat out here. An old-timer replied that he had always found favor with "Rabbit a la Planke." The greenhorn asked what that might be and the old-timer replied, "Well, you take a jack rabbit and skin him out. You stretch him out in front of the fire on a plank until he is toasted a golden brown. Then you carefully take him off the plank, throw him away, and eat the plank."

Anyone who has tried to eat a jack rabbit will recognize that old-timer's words to be good advice. And any old-timer who reads the next passage will also recognize it to be faithful observation:[45]

Old Jerry Downs, out in California, was reading the news to some half a dozen of his neighbors. He read to them the item of intelligence that the grass was very short on the Plains, and it was feared that the emigrants would fare badly. "Emigrants? What's them?" asked one of the listeners.

"Don't you know?" asked Jerry.

"No."

"Don't you? Don't you? Don't you?" he asked of each in turn, and received from each a negative answer. "Well, I'll tell you. Emigrants is a sort of cross between a ground hog and a gopher and is very bad on grass."

4

SONS OF
THE WEST

How you gonna keep 'em down on the farm, after
they've seen the farm?
> Abe Burrows, as quoted by
> Dick Cavett

Police Court Judge: "Is this true?"
Drunk Defendant: "Well, Judge, it's kinda true."
> Ben Clough

CRIME DOESN'T PAY (but then neither does
agriculture).
> Bumper sticker

By now, surely, I must have convinced you that the
frontier Plains was extraordinary—for better or worse, and
that the creatures the homesteaders encountered or raised
there transcended anything imagined then or now. So what
kind of men and women did it take to handle such conditions? People like you and me? I should say not. They are
generally too modest to say so themselves, but the frontiersmen matched both the scenery and the critters of the Plains
in every fantastic extreme. This is clearly implied by the
publications and oral tales of the time. Take, for example, a
notice that appeared in the *Omaha Bee* on August 30,
1886:[1]

Tall men will command high wages reaching for the
corn crop this fall.

There is substantial evidence suggesting that the process
that selected those who would be content to stay at home in
comfort combined with the process determining who would

survive rather than turning the wagon tongue eastward; the results were, to put it modestly, striking. That may seem to the casual reader from somewhere other than the Plains to be a naked boast, but once again the historian or anthropologist cannot turn his back on the clear documentary evidence that has accumulated in the *government supervised* files of the WPA's Federal Writers Project![2]

> The festivities at the cowboy tournament at Hyannis the other day were eminently pleasing and satisfactory. The Governor, with the members of his cabinet, arrived in response to an invitation, and instead of standing supinely by, with a bored look on their faces, they manfully took part in the exercises and helped to entertain the crowd, thereby winning the most enthusiastic praise. There was an old buckskin broncho on the grounds which had been tackled in vain by the most expert cowboys in that region; none of them could break the animal, and consequently when Governor Savage announced that he would ride that broncho or break a leg trying, the people tried to dissuade him, but he would not listen to their arguments. "I have never yet seen the pony, cow, or merry-go-round that I couldn't ride," said the governor, firmly but respectfully; he then vaulted to the back of the desperate animal, which had neither saddle nor bridle upon it, and the ensuing scene was too painful for a detailed description. Spectators say that there seemed to be a whole herd of buckskin bronchos ridden by the forty-eight governors, and the noise and dust, and creaking of timbers, and rending of garments, were frightful. When the smoke of battle had cleared away, and the people could see distinctly what was going on, they found that the governor was still on top, comparatively uninjured, but the broncho was a wreck. His Excellency had kicked in several of its ribs and had pulled out its tail, and was going to use it for a whip, and the ends of its wishbone were sticking out of its ears. It was the greatest feat of horsemanship ever seen at Hyannis and the applause was deafening.

On the other hand, some of the pioneers attributed their sturdy condition not so much to their own breeding or to the climate or soil as to the remarkable state of science on the frontier:[3]

I was unfortunate enough to fall down the elevator shaft of the Burr Block. My feelings as I descended, passing floor after floor, and recognizing the offices of friends, who little dreamed of the tragedy that was in progress so near them—my feelings, I say, may be better imagined than described.

When I reached the bottom and struck the floor with sickening violence, I was accosted by a representative of Dr. Geewhillikens, the eminent physician and scientist, who urged me to take at once three bottles of the doctor's Diamond Dope, and this I did, hardly conscious of the act, so great was my misery.

Scarcely had I swallowed the miraculous Diamond Dope, however, than all the pain left me, and I walked seven miles, and whipped a man named Robinson, and sawed a cord of wood, and threw an anvil over the University. How can I express my gratitude to Dr. Geewhillikens, or my appreciation of the Diamond Dope? All I can do is to urge those who have fallen down elevator shafts, or been run through threshing machines, to give the wonderful medicine a trial, and they will live to bless the grand old doctor, as I do now.

Certainly the frontiersman's ingenuity, which I have praised before in these pages, was a major part of this success, and there is no lack of documented examples of the brilliant combination of imagination and genius leading to profitable results on the pioneer Plains. Two frinstances:[4]

"I want to tell you a little story about my boy out in Newbraskey," said an old farmer in the smoking car to a party of drummers who had been telling him some pretty tall yarns. "My boy is a good deal of a genius in his way, lemme tell you, and one of them gets away with him. T'other day he rigged up a kite. It was the biggest kite I'd ever set eyes on. It was about six feet wide, and twice as long, an' on the top of it my boy placed a few green branches which he cut from a cottonwood tree.

" 'What's them for?' I inquired. 'Never you mind, Dad,' says he. 'I know what I'm about,' and by gosh he did. He flew that kite up in the air and stood watchin' it for a long time, and I says to him, 'You'd better pull that big thing down an' get to your work.' 'Limme alone, Dad,' he replied, 'I'll get there yet,' and, by gosh, he did.

"The next time I took a look at him he was a-haulin' in on the kite line with a smile on his face as big as a furrer[?]. When the kite came down near the ground I saw what he was smilin' at, an' it was enough to make a body smile too. Any you fellers want to guess what was on that kite?"

None of the drummers wanted to guess, and the old man continued his story.

"Wal, sir, a-sittin' on the top o' that kite was eleven of the purtiest wild geese ye ever saw. Yessir, eleven of 'em. You see, the geese was flyin' north purty thick an' my boy got up this scheme to catch 'em. There ain't many trees out our way, an' after a fat goose has been flyin' purty steady all day he gits kind o' tired like an' looks around for a place to sit down and rest. By offerin' the geese a place to stop and rest, and by smearing the top of the kite with tar so their feet would stick so fast they couldn't git away, he did the business. By Gosh! But it was fun to pull them geese in. Just as fast as we could send the kite up and pull her down again we got ten to a dozen geese, an' I'm takin' 'em to Chicago now to sell. None o' you smart story-tellin' fellers don't happen to know what wild geese is worth in Chicago market, do you?"

"There are some mighty green men in this world," said the passenger from the West, "and I struck one of 'em a week or two ago. If I hadn't, I wouldn't be here now. Last Spring I went out into western Nebraska and homesteaded a quarter section. I hadn't seen the land, but took it supposin' it was all right. But when I got there I found it already inhabited. About 150 acres of the 160 were covered with a prairie-dog town. Well, I concluded to settle down and see what I could do, and I'm mighty glad now that I did. About two weeks ago I was up to the railroad station trying to get trusted for some bacon and flour and terbacker, an' feelin' right smart discouraged. I was out of money and grub, and winter was comin' on fast, and I couldn't see any way out of it but to eat prairie dogs, and they're mighty hard to catch. But that day was the turning point in my luck. While I was at the station an Englishman got off the cars, and said as how he was out lookin' for a place to make an investment. Said he'd heard of the fur business, an' wanted to know if he was out in the fur country yet. 'Furs,' says I, 'There ain't nothing . . . ,' but just then an idea struck me, and I changed my tune. 'Furs,' says I, 'There ain't no better fur country than this on earth. Just come out to my place till I show you my fur farm.'

"And he went out with me, an' I showed him the prairie-dog town, an' as luck would have it, it was a bright sunny day. And the dogs was out scootin' around by the hundreds.

" 'Talkin' about furs,' says I, 'what d'ye think of that? I've been six months growin' those mink, an' hain't sold a spide [sic]. It's all natural grease. Guess they's about seven thousand of them now an' they double every year. How many will there be in ten years?'

"You oughter seen the Englishman's eyes open as he took out his pencil an' figured it up. He made it 7,168,000 mink.

" 'Well,' says I, 'I call it 5,000,000 to be on the safe side. It won't cost $1 to keep 'em either, an' if they're worth one dollar a piece, there's millions in it.'

"Then we got down to business, and in less than an hour I had sold out for $7,000 cash, and the next I paid $320 for the homestead at the land office, got my patent, transferred it to him and took the first train for the East. Step into the buffer with me, partner, and take a drink."

The 19th-century homesteader was not at all, on the other hand, the high-minded, idealistic fellow he is frequently depicted to have been. He had to walk a mile to water in a good many cases, which reduced bath-taking to a bare necessity, so to speak, and he wasted little time on primping and grooming. The *Hebron Journal* for September 23, 1875,[5] carried a story about the local barber who, as he was trimming the locks of one of the local settlers, ran upon something hard with his scissors, which turned out to be a whetstone that the farmer had put behind his ear while sharpening his scythe during the haying season the July before!

The work was hard, harder than now, in fact, for no job was avoided just because it seemed too difficult on the surface:[6]

A story that has been going the rounds for a few days past that Jim Dunn and Judge Wild had bought the Black Hills and intended to move them to Dewitt turns out to be a mistake. The gentlemen thought to encircle the Hills with a cable log chain, hitch Wild's mule to the chain, and snake them away. The difficulty of crossing the Platte without building a special bridge was so great that they have abandoned the undertaking.

Of course there were laggards and slugabeds too but even they contributed to the general advance of knowledge and technology by applying their particular virtue to new concepts of efficiency: some enterprising Plainsmen found, for example, that there were all manner of advantages to making huge buckwheat pancakes just before retiring for the evening. The pancakes were put on the bed piping hot, where they served through the night as a fine comforter and in the morning as a fast and convenient breakfast.[7]

"Arkansas" Bob Gillispie was the subject of a good many Nebraska Sandhills tall tales, for, like so many cowboys, he was prepared for anything at all as long as he was permitted the use of a good horse and a length of rope. He used to tell one on himself, about the time a friend told Arkansas Bob that he wanted his house moved and Bob volunteered to handle the job single-handedly. Everyone scoffed of course but Bob tossed his rope around the house and set his horse to pulling the building right down the street. Bob was surprised when he noticed that his horse was sweating after only a half mile but he found the obvious explanation when he finally got the house to its new location five miles away: he was not only pulling the house but the basement too![8]

Despite the press of work and the environment the Plains pioneer indulged himself in the arts and achieved new levels of accomplishment there too:[9]

> A man has painted a dog so natural that the animal had the hydrophobia during the hot weather. He's the same man that painted a copy of a beer-bottle with such skill that the cork flew out just as he was finishing it. And after he was married, he painted a picture of his first baby so lifelike that it cried, and his wife spanked it before she discovered her mistake.

The motif of the realistic picture—real beyond the

bounds of credulity—was a theme of special popularity on
the Plains frontier:[10]

> An American lately in London who was badgered by
> the English on almost every topic, at last determined to
> go on the Mississippi steamboat style, and brag down
> everything. His first chance occurred at an exhibition of
> paintings, where a picture of a snowstorm attracted gen-
> eral admiration. "Is not that fine?" asked a John Bull.
> "Could you show anything as natural as that in
> America?"
>
> "Pooh!" answered the free-born American, "that is
> no comparison to a snowstorm picture painted by a cous-
> in of mine a few years since. That painting was so natu-
> ral, Sir, that a mother who incautiously left her babe
> sleeping in a cradle near it, on returning to the room,
> found her child frozen to death."

If the Plainsmen had bothered to patent half of their
brilliant inventions the Washington Patent Office would be
three times its present size, I have been told. Yet how wonderful it would be if more of the results of pioneer genius
were not lost to us today. For example, a baker of the time
invented a new kind of yeast that made bread so light that a
pound of it weighed only twelve ounces.[11]

Admittedly, an item like that displays more ingenuity
of invention in the telling than in the fact, but quite
honestly—if I may be forgiven such a digression in this
volume—there were actual examples of ingenuity that rival
the tall tale, even in truth:[12]

> When cars were really new things, kids used to get
> under the bridge and drive nails up through the planks.
> And they'd puncture the tires. Farmers couldn't afford
> new tires so they'd fill the tires with oats and then soak
> 'em with water and they'd swell up and make the tire
> tight.

Yet another example of the fantastic in truth: politics
has always been noted for exaggeration in the class of the
tall tale, but few have accused politicians of having a sense
of humor or exercising truly interesting inventiveness. A
Nebraska bloc did combine deviousness with an admirable
sense of the new approach:[13]

. . . The state [Nebraska] adopted the idea [of a one house legislature] in 1934, the same year that parimutuel betting on horse races was approved by the voters. Some said, acidly, that the Omaha gamblers, not confident that their voters could differentiate between two such alien words . . . ordered them to vote for both. Both won.

But the line between the clever mind and the cutting wit is thin. It may not exist at all, that line. For example, the lesson of this next item cannot be denied and yet there is a curiously troublesome obviousness about it:[14]

To keep skippers out of bacon in the summer, eat it in the early spring.

I was once working with a friend of mine from Germany and we were in a tight fix of some sort. I suggested a simple course of action that avoided the problem rather than solving it. My friend Konrad mumbled under his breath, "An American solution," and that is precisely true, and a compliment of the first water. "An American solution," the easy road, the clever path, the surprising path to success and victory. Here are some examples of what I have come to regard proudly as "American solutions" from the Plains frontier:[15]

The first actress to appear in Virginia City was Antoinette Adams, variously described as six feet tall, long-necked, Roman-nosed, crack-voiced, and a faded blonde. Although her audience of miners was cruelly disappointed in what they saw and heard, they listened patiently through her first rendition. At the first pause in her performance, a burly miner stood up and ordered the audience to give three cheers for "Aunty." The cheers resounded, and Antoinette sang again. Once more the miners applauded her, then one man rose to suggest they give her enough money to retire from her profession. A shower of silver cascaded upon the stage, the audience rowdily saluting her retirement. After that, every time Antoinette opened her mouth to sing, the miners cheered her so lustily she could not be heard; they also hurled more silver at her feet. At last the actress surrendered and ordered the curtains pulled. When she gathered the silver up, it filled two money sacks. But Antoinette could take a hint: she left town the next day.

***

At a Methodist meeting the singer who led the psalm
tune, finding that the concluding word, which was Jacob,
had not syllables enough to fill up the music adequately,
ended thus: "Ja-a-a—Ja-a-a—tol de riddle-cob!"

In the East the newswriters continued to view the
Western bumpkin as an incorrigible fool, but the fact of the
matter was that the Westerners knew they were joking,
while the New York writers didn't know 1) that the tale
was a joke, 2) that the Westerner despite his straight face
was laughing, 3) that he was laughing at the Easterner as
well as the joke, and 4) that the Easterner never knew that
the Westerner knew that the Easterner never knew:[16]

The manner in which they weigh a hog out West, it
is said, is to put the hog in one scale and some stones in
the other and then guess at the weight of the stones.

It can perhaps be explained by the canons of practical-
ity, expediency, efficiency, or pragmatism but never ignorance, this frontier sense of humor. What a splendid view
of reality resides in the world understanding that permits an
exchange like this one:[17]

A census taker approaches a sod house during the
early years of settlement on the Plains and is busy count-
ing kids. Even though the mother and father had reported
there being thirteen kids he finds only twelve.

"What happened to the other child?" he asks.

"Fell down the two-holer this morning." came the
astonishing reply.

"Well, why don't you fish him out?"

"We can make a new one easier than we can clean
up that one."

Certainly that the bulk of these improvisations is not
around for our benefit today is because what even then
seemed wise in theory simply did not always work out
advantageously in the fact. It was reported[18] for instance
that an early settler in Nebraska invented a rifle with an
exceedingly long range—but it turned out that the game
shot with it would spoil long before the hunter could arrive
to retrieve it.

This same breed of firearm developed such a ferocious
recoil that if it was hard on the pioneers it is clear that it

would certainly be unendurable for Modern Man: A group of pioneer Nebraskans were once matching stories about kicking guns—[19]

"Talk about guns kicking! Why, I had my collarbone broken twice, my shoulder knocked out of place, and my shoulder blade smashed to smithereens. I don't think now a gun kicks unless it turns my shoulder around to the middle of my back."

A fellow just in from the rural districts looked askance at the speaker and with a twinkle in his eye said, "I was out huntin' with my old musket t'other day when a flock of geese flew over my head. I just put the old fire-piece on my shoulder and banged away. Land sakes, how the air was filled with feathers! And that gun kicked so hard that it knocked both my ankles out of joint!"

The silence that ensued was so dense that you had to cut your way out of it.

Curiously, while the frontier managed to deal successfully with all manner of hardship and mastered virtually every new technological device that came along, from patent postholes sold through the catalogue to board stretchers, the automobile proved to be a constant vexation and contributed substantially to the eventual demise of the Great American Desert, the frontier, and the pioneer spirit:[20]

A farmer started to town with his machine the other day. He had his back seat loaded with wheat in sacks. Just as he was passing a stubble field his steering gear broke and his machine went wild. Before he could get control of it, it had leaped the fence and plowed up the stubble field and sowed the wheat all over the ground. The farmer fell out and got caught under the machine and the machine drug the ground with him covering up the wheat.

It then tore over the field and killed about fourscore of blackbirds that were trying to undo the auto's strenuous efforts. Finally it got headed for a piece of timberland and cleared the ground tearing up stumps and all. A big fat steer was knocked over and killed. The machine tore the hide off of him and hung his carcass in a tree to cool. By this time the gasoline was running low and the machine became exhausted entirely. Then it stopped and the farmer crawled out and started looking for a monkey wrench.

"Today's Man is dogged and determined too!" you insist, and of course you are right. We can struggle single-mindedly until we arrive at a final goal, but I doubt seriously that we can nonetheless maintain the flexibility of the Plains pioneer. He moved fixedly toward an end, I admit, but he remained flexible too, as I have insisted before in these pages. He was always prepared to shift his strategies and if necessary direct his efforts in a new direction.

An old-timer once told me[21] that he had been fishing up in the Sandhills lakes—or at least was trying to fish, but he could not find any bait. He tried catching frogs, but every time he reached for one it would jump way out into the water. So he just waited until the next time the sun went under a cloud and he clapped his hands; the frogs all jumped for the water and the second the sun went under the cloud the lake froze, and there were all those frogs frozen down in the ice with their legs sticking up. He decided to forget the fishing, however, went home for a lawn mower and mowed off the frogs' legs. They ate frog legs for nearly three weeks.

It is this quality of unbridled flexibility that permitted the Plains frontiersman to survive, I believe. It is flexibility that is the essence of the "American Solution." What do you do when the homesteading laws require a window in your house—but there are no windows to be bought and no money to buy them with if there were windows?[22]

"They build 'dobies' on Prairie Creek with only one window, and that's the chimney."

What do you do if you are running a newspaper in the middle of nowhere, where there is no help, no paper, no ink, and no one who can read, no one who has the money to buy a paper if they could read?[23]

Our paper is two days late this week . . . owing to an accident to our press. When we started to run the press Wednesday night, as usual, one of the guy ropes gave way, allowing the forward glider fluke to fall and break as it struck the flunker flopper. This, of course, as anyone who knows anything about a press will readily understand left the gang-plank with only the flip-flap to support it, which also dropped and broke off the wooper-chock. This loosened the fluking from between the ranrod and the flibber-snatcher, which also caused trouble. The report that the delay was caused by the over-indulgence in stimulants by ourselves, is a tissue of falsehoods, the peeled appearance of our right eye being caused by our going into the hatchway of the press in our anxiety to start it, and pulling the coupling pin after the slap-bang was broken, which caused the dingus to rise up and welt us in the optic. We expect a brand-new glider fluke on this afternoon's train.

And what do you do if you are running a newspaper and there are complaints of no news—mostly because there is no news?[24]

A western editor, whose subscribers complained very loudly that he did not give them news enough for their money, told them that if they did not find enough in the paper they had better read the Bible, which, he had no doubt, would be news to most of them.

And, finally, what do you do when you are ready to give up? There's not a tree to hang yourself from, nowhere to buy poison, no shells for the rifle, no water to drown in, nothing higher than a hay bale to leap from? Well, you consider an item like the following, laugh, and get ready to face another rainless day:[25]

A recent California paper contains a letter from Frederick Lichtenberger, M.D., who states that a companion named Ernest Fluchterspiegel, while prospecting for gold in the neighborhood of Frazer River, found some "geodes," which are masses of quartz containing a pint of fluid called the "water of crystallization," which was drank by the unfortunate man, with a jesting remark; and soon after he complained of great weight and pain in his stomach and bowels. In a short time he died, and his body instantly became rigid, and in a few hours petrification took place, the whole body—flesh, blood, heart, liver, intestine, etc. becoming stone. Thus, by drinking half a pint, the poor fellow became quartz.

It is the American Solution. You don't attack a problem that offers no easy footholds; you simply laugh at it, ignore it as best as possible, go around it, try to forget it. These years on the Plains, when cattle raisers are going broke by the tens of dozens and the economy seems on the edge of ruin, they tell of two brothers in the cattle-feeding business—well, not exactly in the business. The one steals cattle and the other steals feed, and they are still losing forty dollars a head on sale.

Nonetheless, despite apparent setbacks like that, the true frontiersmen always assumed the best:[26]

It is the opinion of a western editor that wood goes further when left out-of-doors than when well housed. He says some of his went half a mile.

Or—[27]

A printer in Arkansas, whose office is ten miles from any other building, and who hangs his sign on a limb of a tree, advertises for an apprentice. He says, "A boy from the country preferred."

Or—[28]

A man out West, who offered bail for a friend, was asked by the judge if he had any encumbrance on his farm. "Oh yes," said he, "my old woman."

But *principles* were seldom compromised. What was right was right, and wrong was wrong, wherever found, under any circumstances. William Jennings Bryan, a famous Nebraskan, was a stern opponent of the gold standard for our monetary system; his "Cross of Gold" speech was a classic. And his support for a silver standard was, to say the least, strong among his Nebraska constituency. It was reported[29] that one fellow in Crete, Nebraska, was so stalwart on the silver question that he dug up all the goldenrod and marigolds in the garden, raised only white corn, wouldn't speak to his wife because she had golden hair, was forever denouncing the gold cure, won't keep the golden rule, and refused upon death to enter the golden gates.

Now, I would not like to leave you with the impression that the pioneers were unthinking supporters of political figures. Indeed, they displayed a candor toward such that we could use a liberal dose of today:[30]

Not many years ago—but before Lincoln, the capital,

had an existence—the Governor (Butler) was stumping the state (where a stump is a great rarity), and as darkness came on ere his destination was reached, he halted for the night at the hut of a hardy pioneer; and, as room was scarce, the Governor was assigned to a bed with Pat. As they were preparing for the couch the Governor said, "Well, Pat, you'd live a long time in the Old Country before you could sleep with a governor."

"Yes," said Pat, "and it would be a longer time afore the likes of ye wud be Governor!"

There was not only an absence of class distinction on the frontier; that absence was ferociously exercised and defended. Newcomers who expected any sort of consideration by virtue of their station in the Old Country were liable to be just as surprised, or more so, than Governor Butler. The following narrative is from Wyoming cowboy lore:[31]

I was cook for an outfit that was owned by two sons of an English Lord. Their foreman was an American and was under contract to the two Britishers for a term of three years.

One day the foreman was talking to me when the Englishmen rode up and dismounted. I went on about my work because I knew that the Englishmen had come to talk to the foreman, but I was in hearing distance and I heard one of the Britains say to the foreman, "You will have to bow when you meet us."

The foreman replied, "I don't bow to any man."

"But we are the sons of English lords!"

"Well, sons of lords and sons of bitches are all the same in this country."

The Englishmen paid him three years' salary and fired him.

If they hadn't fired him for his honesty, the foreman probably would have quit out of his own sense of integrity!

It was in fact precisely this candor—unashamed, unadorned honesty—that marked pioneer humor and attitudes. Witness this story recorded as being from Nebraska—[32]

"Why Charlie, where do you expect to go when you die if you talk in this way?"

"Well, Ma," replied this young son of the West, "I guess I'll go to my funeral."

To which an editor of the *Harpers New Monthly Magazine* commented, "After that, conversation lagged."

I have always admired the well-thought-out reply of the Kansan who was being challenged about why he and his military comrades of the state militia had deserted an important position under fire and attack:[33] "Well, we couldn't hardly take it with us!"

But then military life with all its airs and nonsensical formality never did sit well on the pioneer mentality.[34]

An officer of the regular army, Lt. Manus of the 10th Infantry, recently met with a sad rebuff at Fort Kearny, Nebraska Territory. The Lieutenant was promenading in full uniform one day and approaching the sentinel (volunteer) was challenged with "Halt! Who comes there?"

The lieutenant, with contempt in every lineament of his face, expressed his ire with an indignant, "Ass!"

The sentry's reply, apt and quick, came "Advance, Ass, and give the countersign."

And yet when it came down to the raw task of fighting, they apparently were second to none, as is suggested by this item from an eastern publication:[35]

"What regiment is that?" asked a soldier, as a regiment of blood-thirsty Nebraskans were marching by.

"The One Hundred and Last Nebraskan," remarked a warrior.

"I thought so," said another warrior. "Heard the government didn't want any more Nebraska troops!"

The insistence on straight-forward truth is exemplified in one of the most popular stories of the 19th century. A plainsman and an eastern visitor, it seems, were riding across the prairie on a bitter cold winter day. The visitor asked the shivering sodbuster why he didn't wear his buffalo robe with the fur-side in. "Do you suppose that the buffalo didn't know how to wear his own hide?" was the indignant rejoinder.[36]

Yet such attitudes are not contradictions of the ingenuity I have already outlined. It is simply that the homesteader would not let himself be bound by the arbitrary limits of a system of logic being imposed on him:[37]

Dakota, as well as other places in the Federal baili-wick, is entitled to her place in the Drawer in words fol-lowing, to wit: A fellow who had solemnly pledged himself not to drink a drop of liquor inside or outside of a house in two years was passing a saloon in Elk Horn where three companions were having a glass, and he could not but cast a wistful glance at the scene. One of them spied him and asked him to join them. "Oh no," said he, "I wish I could but I've sworn not to take a drop either inside a house or outside for two years."

"Oh," says one, "You can have one drink for all that. We'll lift you off the threshhold and you can have one drink half inside the house and half out."

So one took hold of each leg, and thus they raised him up, while the third filled and passed the bottle. He took one long drink, and was just drawing breath for another when one of his supporters shifted a little, and he shouted, "Oh, hold me even, boys; my soul's in your hands!"

Time and space, other arbitrary systems, were treated in a cavalier fashion under certain circumstances. One of my favorite stories is told by Oscar Henry of Colorado Springs, a long-time observer of the scene on the Plains and a man of particular eloquence. He tells of a little boy who became angry one afternoon after some slight or another; he announced to his family that he was running away. He packed up a few essentials and made it out to the barn before he settled down to think things over. After an hour or so, when the sun began to go down, he decided to make a dramatic return to the bosom of his home.

He came in just as the family was beginning dinner, and no one paid much attention to his arrival. "Well," he said after a few moments had passed without his being noticed, "I see you still have the same old cat."

That sort of laconic delivery, the most stunning kind of understatement, was also lost on the eastern sophisticates. All they could see was the blank, unmoved face of the joker; the humor was lost on them:[38]

A western gent, at the St. Nicholas, the other day,

having taken possession of his room, locked it up to go out into the city, and leaving the key at the bar told the clerk with great simplicity "not to wait dinner for him."

Did the editor in the following item seriously propose these spellings or was he, as I suspect, pulling the leg of those Eastern editors who considered spelling to be such an all-fired important matter?[39]

A western editor thinks that if the proper way of spelling tho is though and ate eight and bo beau, the proper way of spelling potatoes must be poughteighteaux. The new way to spell softly is psoughtleigh.

My conscience bothers me considerably whenever I use the words "tall tale" or worse yet "lies" in reference to any pioneer accounts because by nature they were in reality brutally true. "Plain language" was as complimentary a phrase as one could use to describe another's manner of speaking. John G. Neihardt, the greatest of Plains poets, wrote in his early book *The River and I*[40] that he and his comrades were running out of gas during a long trip down the Missouri River through the Dakotas. Supply sources were few and far between but they knew that they had to find gasoline somewhere or it would be a long trip indeed. He and his companions stopped at a prairie way station to inquire about fuel, but the proprietor had to tell them, "You can't get no gasoline short o' Milk River, and you sure got to paddle, so you better buy whiskey."

In the same blunt vein, there is the story of the Colorado miner who left his companions and was somehow killed.[41] His body was found on the Plains, mutilated by wild beasts. One of the crew of friends was elected to "break the news gently" to the bereaved parents and so, as the account goes, ". . . He showed himself equal to the occasion" by penning the following diplomatic message:

Mister Smith
Deer Sur.
The kiotes has ete yur sun's hed off.
                    Yurs
                    John Jones

During the heady moments when I sip good full-malt

Scotch and roll Plains humor around in my head, trying to invent some particularly catchy new analysis of it, I find myself eventually getting around to something like "Style/Execution." That's not a new idea but it is, I guess, quite true; the problem for me is to present that dichotomy in a meaningful way—like the old-timer who married a woman who had been widowed three times before: he knew what to do but didn't quite know how to make it interesting.

The style depended in large part on diction and vocabulary. What pioneer humor says is sometimes not funny because of what it says but rather the way it says it. The humor, that is to say, lies not within the actions described but rather within the words describing the action or responding to it, for example:[42]

> A favorite story, told to illustrate western prices, concerned a Denver housewife who rebelled at the high cost of candles. When the merchant apologized, telling her that the Indian troubles on the Plains kept freight rates high, she snapped, "What?! Are the Indians fighting by candlelight?"

The language of the West and of the frontier have never ceased to be a wonder to outsiders, perhaps because the language was a portable symbol of the romantic reality of the Old West, perhaps because for all its rough edges it constitutes an American oral literature:[43]

> The dialect of the West is rather strong, and slightly hyperbolical. One Brown, who has lately been traveling in the Occident, as far as Arkansas, says that when a man in that region desires to say that he would like a drink, he declares that if he had a glass of whiskey he would throw himself outside of it, mighty quick!

That last example is more revealing than the story itself. Note how the New York editor has laced the narrative with two-dollar words, elaborated and explained, hung geegaws and fooferaws, finials and furbelows on every vacant piece of prose, much in the nature of Victorian architecture. What a contrast then the economy of pioneer comment is (or for that matter, the soddie, log cabin, or tipi to its eastern analogue). A good deal of western frontier

humor plays on that geographical contrast: the eastern traveler remarks at length on the absence of people on the
Plains and notes that there are actually more cows than
humans, to which the frontiersman responds tersely, "We
prefer 'em," or perhaps the traveler addresses himself to the
remarkable number of hogs in the area and speculates that
perhaps hogs pay better dividends at the market than wheat
or corn, to which the laconic Plainsman comments, "Don't
need to hoe hogs." Indeed, the western frontier tale is not
unlike poetry in the value it puts on the encapsulation of as
much truth as possible in the fewest words:[44]

> An Indiana man bet ten dollars that he could ride a
> fly-wheel in a saw mill, and as his widow paid the bet,
> she remarked, "William was a kind husband, but he
> didn't know much about fly-wheels."

Sometimes it is a remarkable combination of the
humor of the situation and the word formulations that
work together to develop the humor of the frontier tale. An
example of this phenomenon:[45]

> . . . It was during a fall roundup attended by all of
> the cattle owners in the area that a camp was made near
> the town of Douglas. The campsite was located close by
> an old graveyard with many deep, sunken graves. Most of
> the men went into town to celebrate, when night came
> on, and among these was Jerky Bill.
> Returning in the wee, small hours, Bill missed his
> way to camp and upon dismounting his horse stumbled
> into one of the old sunken graves. Too drunk to rise he
> simply slept there until dawn, and, at daybreak, the men
> at the camp heard a great whooping and shouting.
> Rushing to the spot they discovered Jerky Bill sitting
> up in the grave. "Whoopee," he shouted, "Whoopee! It's
> Resurrection Mornin', *and I'm the first one up!*"

Because the cowboy has always been such an object of
romantic adoration a good bit of his diction has been saved
for us too, and capitalized on in the figure of the Silent
Hero of the Silver Screen. I argue then that it is not so
much a matter of cowboy language being that much better
than that of the settler, but more of the best of it has been
passed on to us:[46]

Jim Swisher was shipping some cattle to Omaha and asked me to go along. I accepted the invitation readily. When we reached Omaha of course we had a couple of drinks—maybe one or two too many. But we were carrying them all right when we went into a restaurant and there was a man at a table next to us who had just received his order for fresh oysters, so we ordered oysters.

Then the man began to prepare his oysters to eat and put a drop of some hot potpourri on each one. Jim looked at him out of the corner of his eye and when Jim's oysters arrived Jim picked up the bottle of potpourri and soused a lot of the mixture on his oysters. I nudged him and said, "Not too much, Jim, not too much."

Jim kept on sousing his oysters with the hot stuff and said, "Hell, if a little is good, a lot is better."

Then Jim put an oyster in his mouth. I watched him out of the corner of my eye and I never have seen anything funnier. Jim clamped his jaws tight on the oyster, then looked around as if he would find a means of escape, then he opened his mouth, then closed it again, and then the tears began to run down his face. The man next to us, who happened to be the only customer in the restaurant besides ourselves, looked at Jim with a puzzled expression.

Of course it takes lots longer to tell than it took to happen. Jim just put the oyster in his mouth, shut his mouth, opened it again, looked around the room in desperation, shut his mouth again, and then his eyes began to water.

And then without more ado, he rose to his feet, grabbed the offending oyster, and throwing it across the room yelled, "Blaze, you son of a bitch, blaze."

Fancy food, from the literary evidence, appears to have always been a problem for the cowpoke. He spent weeks and months, after all, growing used to the cooking of one man and then, just when he had the money to do it up right, he was in some strange place, with a new cook, and menu items he'd never even heard of, yet lusted after:[47]

One cowboy on a visit to town saw a sign reading:
Snack—two bits
Square meal—four bits

> Bellyache—one dollar

He entered the establishment and, when the waitress came up, ordered a dozen rotten eggs and some weak coffee. The waitress thought he was crazy, but the waddie explained that he had a tapeworm and he'd be doggoned if he was going to feed it first-class chuck.

The whiskey drinking habits of the westerners were often blamed on the conditions of the frontier: there was too much distance to haul corn and so it was converted into the much more portable and potable whiskey, and there was little time to be wasted on getting drunk in a civilized manner and thus hard whiskey provided an efficient short-cut. Perhaps that is also the rationale for western language— and even frontier justice. There was no time for the civilized fixings:[48]

> Montanans came to resent all of the road agents working the gold roads. A sizeable number of highway-men, including their leader Plummer, were, as the saying went, "jerked to Jesus." Some of the more humanitarian natives had qualms about this kind of justice and, after one execution, a fellow townsman asked the vigilante who had fitted the noose: "Did you not feel for the poor man as you put the rope around his neck?"
>
> "Yes," replied the hangman sympathetically, "I felt for his left ear."

The other side of the case, as I have outlined it, is that humor which lies within the action rather than within the specific word. Since I have suggested that at least a part of the content of the humor of the frontier lies within the brevity of the statement, it seems altogether fitting and appropriate that now we turn our critical eye toward that prime exponent of inflated language and empty rhetoric, the politician:[49]

> In the early days of Wisconsin, when this State was nearly a wilderness, Colonel Blank moved into these parts, and soon became a noted character. He had one particular failing, so common to most of our Western man, that of spreeing it considerably. One winter, when he represented Iowa County in our Territorial Legislature, he remained under the weather nearly the whole time, and till the close of the season. But the next day after the

session had adjourned the Colonel was found up and dressed, and perfectly sober. One of his co-legislatives accidentally meeting him inquired of him the cause of this, as it was usual for most of them to have a spree after the session. The Colonel very blandly replied that during the session he had represented his constituents; the session having closed, he represented himself.

The process of pioneer enterprise is not unlike a goat's ears: totally unlikely, strangely inappropriate for ears, so totally suitable for a goat. The bizarre circumstances of the American frontier demanded similarly unusual and yet functional responses, responses that in their reality approach the tall tale in dimensions. A man in Colorado, for example, just didn't like the idea of taking a job tending bar during the gold rush days, so he took apart a pair of gloves he had, used the pieces as patterns and made a fortune selling his gloves at nine dollars a pair![50] Entrepreneurs could clean up if they happened to strike on just the right, mad enough idea:[51]

Anything for which there was a market went aboard the canvas-topped prairie schooners. A couple of Germans, catering to those of high taste, loaded one wagon with frozen oysters and peddled them along the way at $2.50 a quart. Others carried apples, selling them in Denver for fifteen dollars a bushel. Perhaps the most interesting cargo was a wagonload of cats, shipped to Denver as mousers. The demand for such services was apparently high, for the cat salesman had no difficulty in disposing of his livestock for a handsome profit.

The preponderance of male-oriented tales suggests that perhaps it was in the male population that the talents for humor lay, but that is not at all the case. Most tall-tale contests run by newspapers during the 19th and 20th centuries were won by women contestants—perhaps because they were the only members of the family who could write. Male dominance of these pages stems perhaps from the fact that there were so many more men on the frontier: yet women were not at all ready to take a back seat to male pranksters. Within the past two days I was told a story[52] of a woman who was preparing pies for a church dinner. As was the custom, and still is in my mother's kitchen, leftover dough was rolled out, filled with jelly or jam, and baked as a "thin pie," a special treat for the children. She packaged up her pies for the church and then set the thin pies in a similar package to the side, to be served to the family the next day. Her husband recognized this situation and thought he would play a little trick and thereby assure that he and the children would get the good pies the next day: he switched the packages.

Well, when her plate of ragged and humble "thin pies" appeared on the dessert table among her neighbors' elegant dishes, the housewife was humiliated. Everyone laughed, recognizing what had gone on, and the man thought he had pulled a good one.

He was perhaps a little chagrined the next day when his wife sent him back into the fields in the afternoon, after lunch, with a pie for him and the hands to enjoy during an afternoon rest. He was probably even more chagrined when he cut open the pie—or rather tried to cut open the pie—and discovered that she had gone to the trouble to cook up a special pie just for him. A feather pie.

It is hard to think of the frontiersman as a pessimist. The idea of frontiering suggests boundless optimism, hope, a future, but there *were* the disillusioned, disappointed, and pessimistic:[53]

"Where is your house?" asked a traveler in the depths of one of the "old solemn wildernesses" of the Great West.

"*House?* I ain't got no house."

"Well, where do you *live?*"

"I live in the woods—sleep on the Great Government Purchase, eat raw bear and wild turkey, and drink out of the Mississippi!"

And he added, "It is getting too *thick* with folks about here. You're the second man I have seen within the last month; and I hear there's a whole family come in about fifty miles down the river. I'm going to put out into 'the woods' again."

There were those who refused to recognize that the frontier days would ever come to an end, that "civilization" would ever reach out to them:[54]

It was during the period when pioneers had partially recovered from their early consternation at the idea of such a thing as a steam railroad, at first looked upon as an invention of the devil himself. They had become somewhat reconciled to the idea of such nerve-wracking speed as ten miles an hour, which they had declared to be greater than a gracious Providence ever intended that man should travel on wheels, and the thought of a railroad was slowly becoming an accepted fact. Indeed, at some time in the future, when the good Lord so willed it, a railroad might pass through their own community.

There was one individual in central Illinois, however, who was somewhat inclined to discount things about him, particularly the supposed attractions of his own immediate locality. In his estimation it was no Arcady, and he was, indeed, inclined to adopt a pessimistic attitude toward everything concerning it.

Time came when Dame Rumor began to assert that a railroad would be forthcoming in that community in the immediate future, and the tidings were hurriedly carried to the pessimistic one by his twelve-year-old son.

"A railroad in this God-forsaken place? Why, they won't even survey the line," he declared.

A few months intervened, when the son again approached his father. "Say, Dad, they're surveyin' the line."

"O well," retorted the disgusted father, "they may survey, but they'll never build a grade."

After a further lapse of time the boy approached his father with the latest report. "Say, Dad," he said, "they're a-building a grade."

"Buildin' a grade, eh?" with great scorn. "Well, that's all the good it'll ever do 'em. They'll never lay a tie."

It was not long after this that the boy came running, announcing breathlessly, "Say, Dad, they're a-laying the ties."

This was a poser, but there was no sign of surrender in the parent's manner as he confidently asserted, "Well, they may lay some ties, but they'll never string a rail."

And then, when the ever-watchful offspring had brought the news that they were stringing rails, the prompt reply was, "They may string some rails, but they'll never run a train through."

It was not very long after this that the boy came running to him, one day, with the most stirring news of all, "Say, Dad, they're runnin' a train through."

The calm, unwavering reply of the confident father was, "Well, it may go through, *but it'll never come back.*"

Well, obviously the essence of the frontier was the men and women who were there, who are in some cases still there. I could go on, I suppose, offering examples of their humor of situation, humor of diction, examples of ingenuity and flexibility, instances of the American Solution, but perhaps I have made my case and presented enough evidence to that effect. Enough, after all, is enough. Which reminds me of another story:[55]

There were two boys who had spent quite a bit of time around their older cousins down at the pool hall, and they got to wondering what it was that the big fellows were talking about when they laughed about going over to Mabel's place. So they resolved to save up five dollars and find out for themselves what this was all about. The nature of their economy however meant that they only managed to save up about fifty cents over a period of two weeks and they could see that they would probably never be able to get up five dollars between them. They decided they would just go over to Mabel's with their fifty cents and see what happened.

They knocked at the door and the madam answered, astonished at the sight of the two little boys standing on the porch before her. They announced, "We want some of whatever it is the big boys get here," and handed her the fifty cents.

The unruffled woman reached out, grabbed each of the boys by their ears, banged their heads smartly together three times, and sent them reeling backwards down the porch steps into the dust of the street.

After the minute or so that it took them to recall where and who they were, the one looked over at the other and opined, "I don't think I'm ready for five dollars worth of that."

CONCLUSION

Next to the originator of a good sentence is the first quoter of it.

Ralph Waldo Emerson

Truth is the most valuable thing we have. Let us economize it.

Mark Twain

Brevity is the soul of wit.

Shakespeare

There are only two or three human stories, and they go on repeating themselves as fiercely as if they had never happened before.

Willa Cather

Why would any man write a *second* book about lies and liars? Thoughts of exonerating the pioneer from whatever blots I had put on his record did occur to me, for I imagined thousands of sobbing schoolchildren, ranks of indignant teachers, and a growing fury among Plains chapters of the Gray Panthers should I once again accuse our venerable forefathers of a fundamental dishonesty. I worried that perhaps I had tarnished for some—especially the tender young—the golden image of the Dedicated Pioneer. I had visions of being ridden out of town, pioneer style, on a rail as a scheduled part of the Lincoln-Lancaster County Historical Society's annual pageant, wearing of course a newly macadamized suit of chicken leaves.

I have tried to devise my defense well in advance of the general confusion and bustle of a lynching party. I have thought, for example, that I might offer up my firm conviction that underlying (so to speak) the pioneer sense of humor is a profound respect for truth. The momentary inclination to exaggerate was often tempered by moderation and truth:[1]

One fellow had a particularly good talent for lying and his wife told him that the next time he lied she was going to kick him in the shins just as hard as she could. He was talking with someone about a new barn that a neighbor had built. He said, "Why, that is the most fantastic barn you ever saw. It must be a thousand feet long." And the wife hauled off and kicked him as hard as she could. And he continued without a pause, "And one foot wide."

Or I could cite the story about the pioneer who was telling about the time a bear was chasing him and how he had jumped up to a tree limb thirty feet over his head. When *he* was called down for exaggerating he confessed that he hadn't exactly jumped up to the limb; he caught it on the way down.[2]

But I will never have to use such defenses. My fears have been laid to rest. Hopefully I have cleared away any such illusion of accusation against the pioneers and their narrative ways. If my intention in *Shingling the Fog and Other Plains Lies* was to introduce a new face of the Plains pioneer—the homesteader as liar—then my intention here has been to dwell on the skills of their lying—the *art* and *craft* of prevarication. Far from accusing the frontiersman of lying, I am certifying him as such.

Were our forefathers liars? You bet they were, and damned fine ones at that.

NOTES

Foreword and Introduction

1. Athearn, Robert, *High Country Empire: The High Plains and Rockies* (University of Nebraska Press; Lincoln, 1960), pp. 189, 227.
2. For further information about the sod house, see my *Sod Walls: The Story of the Nebraska Sod House* (Purcells; Broken Bow, Nebraska, 1970).
3. Macmillan; New York, 1964.
4. From "Wise and Otherwise," the magazine's humor column, this extract from I:3, February 21, 1857.
5. From *The American Joe Miller*, a classic jokebook.
6. In the new edition published by Alfred A. Knopf, New York, 1962.
7. *Harpers New Monthly Magazine*, XXV:CXLVI, July, 1862: "Surry County, North Carolina," by "Skitt, who was raised thar."
8. Dobie, Frank, "A Preface on Authentic Liars," *Tall Tales from Texas* by Modie Boatwright (Southwest Press; 1934). Thanks to Dan Newton for finding this one.
9. *Harpers New Monthly Magazine*, CCCCLXXX:LXXX, May, 1890, "The Evolution of Humor," by Prof. S. H. Butcher, LL.D., p. 902.
10. P. xiii.
11. P. xiv.
12. Pp. 3-4.
13. Munchausen had good reason to fear for his life. Americans by this time were sick and tired of the English and Continental travelers of the 18th and 19th centuries who had come to this country, often for short periods of time, enjoyed the hospitality—humble though it might have been—of the citizens, and then rushed back home to write scathing attacks on American manners, morals, and culture—or rather their lack of the same.
14. The American temper and immediate propensity for fighting was of international repute, third only to the disgusting, universal habits of chewing tobacco and trading; in these cases, foreign accounts would have had to be even more preposterous to be libelous.
15. *Harpers New Monthly Magazine*, XXIV:CXLIII, April, 1862,

"The Drawer," p. 714. "The Drawer" was the humor column of the *Harpers New Monthly Magazine*.

16. *Harpers Weekly*, VIII:408, October 22, 1864, p. 683.
17. Athearn, pp. 194, 195.
18. Athearn, p. 186.

Beyond Civilization

1.   Roger L. Welsch, "This Mysterious Light Called an Airship: Nebraska 'Saucer' Sightings, 1897," *Nebraska History*, 60:1, Spring 1979, pp. 92-113.
2.   The poem was reputedly written by J. B. Kronkright of Juanita, Nebraska, and was located without further documentation in the WPA files of the Nebraska State Historical Society, index number 245.7.
3.   From the Nebraska State Historical Society's WPA files, which indicate that this originally appeared in the *Wealth Makers* newspaper (n.1.) on April 18, 1895.
4.   Published as *Tall Stories: The Rise and Triumph of the Great American Whopper* (Funk and Wagnalls Co.; New York and London, 1931).
5.   Athearn, p. 226.
6.   From the Nebraska State Historical Society's WPA files, 243.3, n.1.
7.   *Nebraska Herald*, April 23, 1868; Nebraska State Historical Society WPA files.
8.   Originally published on July 20, 1907; from the Nebraska State Historical Society WPA files, 243.1.
9.   From the Nebraska State Historical Society WPA files, 243.1.
10. *Pawnee Press*, Beatrice, Nebraska, March 11, 1865, from the Nebraska State Historical Society WPA files.
11. *Pawnee Press*, December 10, 1884, cited as "taken from the *Madison Chronicle*."
12. *Harpers Weekly*, "Humors of the Day," XII:621, November 21, 1868, p. 747, and *The Book of Lies*, by John Heaton (Morse; New York, 1896), pp. 143-146, as quoted by B. A. Botkin in *Treasury of American Folklore* (Crown; New York, 1944), pp. 599-600.
13. "Switchel" was any one of a number of formulas designed to quench field hands' thirsts on hot, dusty days. It usually had some molasses, ginger, and vinegar in it and was carried to the fields in a large jug covered with a wet burlap bag.
14. *Weekly Burtonian*, August 1, 1888, as taken from the *Fremont Tribune*; Nebraska State Historical Society WPA files.
15. Both of these tales were collected near Yankton, South Dakota, by Dorothy Shonsey, bless her.

16. As reported in the Sunday *Omaha World-Herald*, November 14, 1971.

17. From an otherwise unidentified document in the Nebraska State Historical Society WPA files.

18. An undocumented, unmarked manuscript from the WPA files of the Nebraska State Historical Society.

19. *Harpers Weekly*, "Humors of the Day," VI: 281, May 17, 1862, p. 307.

20. Louise Pound "Some of the Tall Tales of Nebraska," *Nebraska History*, XXIV:1, January-March, 1943, pp. 57-58.

21. Pound notes, "Through his banking and railroad interests Jay Cooke came to represent to the western farmer all that was ruthless and rapacious; and when the House of Cooke, after much propping up, finally crashed in September, 1873, precipitating a great panic, his name became the symbol of the graft and skullduggery that had impoverished the country."

22. *O'Neill Beacon Light*, May 7, 1897; from Nebraska State Historical Society WPA files, 243.3.

23. *The Opposition* (n.1.), November 29, 1883; from Nebraska State Historical Society WPA files, 243.3.

24. *Chadron Recorder*, November 23, 1894; from Nebraska State Historical Society WPA files, n.n.

25. As reported in the *Lyons Mirror*, August 15, 1895; from Nebraska State Historical Society WPA files, 243.3.
    and
    Tekamah Burtonian, September 10, 1896; from the Nebraska State Historical Society WPA files, 243.3.

26. *The Dodge Criterion*, July 9, 1897; from the Nebraska State Historical Society WPA files, 243.3.

27. Probably from the Gothenburg, Nebraska, *Independent*, but not documented in the Nebraska Historical Society's WPA files.

28. From the WPA files of the Nebraska State Historical Society.

29. From the WPA files of the Nebraska State Historical Society.

30. P. 10, 25.

31. All weather records are taken from the *New York Times Encyclopedic Almanac 1970* (*New York Times*, 1969).

32. See my pamphlet "Of Trees and Dreams" (Nebraska State Forester's Office; Lincoln, 1982).

33. Merrill Mattes, *The Great Platte River Road* (Nebraska State Historical Society; Lincoln, 1961), p. 162.

34. *New Harpers Monthly Magazine*, "Editor's Drawer," XLVIII:CCLXXXVII, April, 1874, p. 764.

35. Russell Meints, for what that's worth.

36. *Omaha Bee*, August 29, 1886; from the Nebraska State Historical Society's WPA files. The great curve of the river mentioned here did exist in fact and was referred to by many travelers, including Lewis and Clark. Now the great curve has been reduced considerably by the straightening of the river bed and stabilization of the shifting banks.
37. Samuel Clemens, *Life on the Mississippi* (H. O. Houghton and Company, 1874 and 1875), p. 136.
38. Athearn, p. 4.
39. Robert J. Burdette, *Gems of Modern Wit and Humor* (L. G. Stahl, 1903), pp. 367-368.
40. Athearn, p. 90.
41. *Harpers New Monthly Magazine*, XIV:LXXIX, December, 1856, p. 142.
42. Charles M. Russell, *Trails Plowed Under* (Doubleday, Page, and Company; Garden City, New York, 1927), pp. 191-194.
43. *Harpers New Monthly Magazine*, XVIII:CV, March, 1859.
44. *Harpers New Monthly Magazine*, XVIII:CVIII, May, 1859.
45. *Harpers New Monthly Magazine*, XXIX:CLXXII, September, 1864.
46. *Harpers Weekly*, "Wise and Otherwise," II:61, February 22, 1858, p. 112.
47. *Harpers Weekly*, "Wise and Otherwise," I:6, February 7, 1857, p. 95.
48. *Harpers New Monthly Magazine*, IX:LIV, November, 1854, p. 851.
49. *Harpers Weekly*, "Humors of the Day," IX:448, July 29, 1865, p. 475.
50. *Harpers New Monthly Magazine*, XVIII:CIV, December, 1849, p. 135.
51. *Harpers Weekly*, II:61, February 27, 1858, p. 114.
52. Mattes, p. 163.
53. *Harpers Weekly*, "Wise and Otherwise," I:15, April 11, 1857.
54. *Harpers New Monthly Magazine*, "Editor's Drawer," LXV:CCCLXXXV, p. 157.
55. *Harpers New Monthly Magazine*, "Editor's Drawer," XLVI:CCLXXIV, March, 1873, p. 639.
56. *Harpers New Monthly Magazine*, "Editor's Drawer," XXX:CLXXIX, April, 1865, p. 676.
57. *Harpers Weekly*, "Humors of the Day," X:494, June 16, 1866, p. 375.
58. *Harpers Weekly*, "Humors of the Day," VII:315, January 10, 1863, p. 18.
59. *Harpers Weekly*, "Wise and Otherwise," I:16, April 18, 1857, p. 255.

60. A variant of this frequently found story appears in the "Humors of the Day" column of the *Harpers Weekly*, XII:591, April 25, 1868, p. 267.

61. *Harpers New Monthly Magazine*, "Editor's Drawer," LXI:CCCLXIII, August, 1880, p. 487.

62. September, 24, from the WPA files of the Nebraska State Historical Society.

63. For those new to Plains history and terminology, the "dugout" was a sod house that was dug back into the side of a hill and fronted with sod or logs. The Sandhills are a series of grass-covered, enormous sand dunes that were blown up centuries ago and have since been "petrified" by the grass that covers them. They cover an enormous area, much larger than many of the smaller states of our union and only a few paved roads go through them. There are farms and ranches in the Sandhills that lie twelve to fifteen miles from any road whatever. There have been efforts to farm the Sandhills but they have usually reverted to grass and are now primarily haying and grazing lands for vast herds of beef cattle. They were opened for homesteading in 1904 but the population "density" is still well below two people per square mile, and dropping.

64. *Oakdale Pen and Plow*, November 3, 1877, from the *Massachusetts Spy*; from the WPA files of the Nebraska State Historical Society.

65. "Wood and Water: Twin Problems of the Prairie Plains," *Nebraska History*, XXIX:2, June, 1948, pp. 87-88.

66. Russell Lord, *Behold Our Land* (Houghton; Boston, 1938), pp. 22, 320, as quoted by B. A. Botkin, p. 332.

67. *The Aurora News*, June 18, 1887; from the WPA files of the Nebraska State Historical Society.

68. Bill Nye, *Bill Nye and Boomerang* (W. B. Conkey Co.; Chicago, 1893).

69. Roger L. Welsch, "No Fuel Like an Old Fuel," *Natural History* (Museum of Natural History, New York), November, 1980.

70. *Valley County Journal*, April 29, 1881, p. 4. Courtesy Lynne Ireland.

71. As told by Gary Fusselman, Lincoln, Nebraska.

72. September, 1869, XXIX:CCXXXIII, p. 623.

Just Summer and Winter

1. Mattes, pp. 97-98.

2. From an unidentified FWP paper labeled "Exciting Episodes in the Early Life of Ananias Woofter," Nebraska State Historical Society. The name "Ananias" is not chosen at random. See the text, page 68.

3. Athearn, p. 226.
4. Anonymous Omaha storyteller.
5. L. A. Jorgensen, Lincoln, Nebraska, in interview.
6. *West Point Progress*, January 20, 1881; from the Nebraska State Historical Society's WPA files.
7. Athearn, p. 171.
8. *Nemaha County Herald*, December 30, 1904; from the Nebraska State Historical Society's WPA files, 243.3.
9. May 20, 1881; from the WPA files of the Nebraska State Historical Society.
10. From "Midlands Scene," October 24, 1971.
11. Marlin Waechter.
12. From *Bill Nye and Boomerang*, pp. 72-74.
13. Bill Nye, *Remarks from Bill Nye* (Thompson and Thomas; Chicago, 1891). "A Mountain Snowstorm," pp. 391-392.
14. From the Nebraska State Historical Society's WPA files.
15. As reported in the *Weekly Burtonian*, July 15, 1887; from the Nebraska State Historical Society's WPA files, 243.3.
16. XXVII:CLXIV, January, 1864, "Editor's Drawer," p. 281.
17. In a personal letter.
18. *Harpers New Monthly Magazine*, VI:XXIV, March 1853, p. 567.
19. This song was one of the most popular folksongs on the Plains during the 19th—and even the 20th—century. Because it so beautifully expressed a people's minds, it was sung as "Sweet Dakota Land," "Sweet Kansas Land," and even "Sweet Saskatchewan." It is filled with glorious ironies: it is sung to the tune of "Beulah Land," when the subject at hand is scarcely that. The adjective "sweet" was not chosen without a sardonic smile. And yet it was sung as a love song. It was never sung by those who were defeated by the Plains; they had few songs. The dry weather version appears in print in my books *Treasury of Nebraska Pioneer Folklore* (University of Nebraska Press; Lincoln, 1966) and *Sod Walls: The Story of the Nebraska Sod House* (Purcells; Broken Bow, Nebraska, 1970); the printed text and my rendition of the song also appears on the album "Sweet Nebraska Land" (Folkways Records, FH5337; New York, 1965).
20. *Harpers Weekly*, II:81, July 17, 1858, p. 454: *Harpers Weekly*, I:3, January 17, 1857, p. 47.
21. Tony Epp, Foreign Language Department, Nebraska Wesleyan University, Lincoln, Nebraska.
22. Collected by Dorothy Shonsey.
23. Both of these tales were collected by Dorothy Shonsey.
24. *Wilsonville, Furnas County Review*, as quoted in the *Chadron Advocate*, August 22, 1890; from the WPA files of the Nebraska State Historical Society.

25. Roger L. Welsch, *The Summer It Rained: Water and Plains Pioneer Humor* (Nebraska Water Resources Center; Lincoln, 1978).

26. Athearn, p. 307; anonymous tale from my own files.

27. From the WPA files of the Nebraska State Historical Society.

28. Dawes County [Nebraska] *Journal*, February 9, 1900; from the WPA files of the Nebraska State Historical Society.

29. Duell, Sloan, and Pearce; New York, 1941.

30. *Republican Journal*, May 12, 1899; from the WPA files of the Nebraska State Historical Society.

31. *Harpers Weekly*, "Humors of the Day," IX:455, September, 9, 1865, p. 367.

32. Unidentified document from the WPA files of the Nebraska State Historical Society.

Catfish at the Pump

1. *The Frontier, Holt County*, July 17, 1924; from the WPA files of the Nebraska State Historical Society, 243.1.

2. Unidentified except for the legend "Week No. 28, item number 51," from the WPA files of the Nebraska State Historical Society.

3. Jaspar Matzke, *This We Remember* (Brodhead, Wisconsin, 1972), p. 15.

4. Stan Hoig, *The Humor of the American Cowboy* (University of Nebraska Press; Lincoln, 1958), 56-57. A "greener" is a greenhorn, a newcomer to the range country.

5. February 16, 1877. Nye was speaking from experience. His mule earned such affection that Nye eventually named both his own newspaper and a book after him, Boomerang, a name obviously chosen for one of the mule's talents. The full title of Nye's book, which is cited above, is *Bill Nye and Boomerang, or The Tale of a Meek-eyed Mule, and Some Other Literary Gems by Bill Nye Himself*.

6. *The Courier*, February 19, 1898; from the WPA files of the Nebraska State Historical Society.

7. Nye, *Bill Nye and Boomerang*, pp. 284-285.

8. *The Weekly Courier*, McCook, Nebraska, December 3, 1896, and the *Ravenna News*, as quoted in the Holt County *Independent*, February 21, 1905; from the WPA files of the Nebraska State Historical Society.

9. *Exchange*, no further data, as quoted in the Tekamah *Burtonian*, November 15, 1883; from the WPA files of the Nebraska State Historical Society.

10. As told to me by an anonymous Nebraska informant.

11. From the WPA files of the Nebraska State Historical Society.

12. Nye, *Bill Nye's Remarks*, pp. 339-340.
13. Nye, *Bill Nye and Boomerang*, pp. 201-202.
14. 1887.
15. This is a tale widely told across the Plains, and, for that matter, throughout the country. A printed variant can be found in Thomas, *Tall Stories*, pp. 19-20.
16. Webb, p. 40.
17. Thomas, p. 26.
18. *Harpers Weekly*, I:21, May 23, 1857, p. 334.
19. XLIX:CCXC, July, p. 303.
20. From *Bill Jones of Paradise Valley, Oklahoma* (J. J. Callison; Kingfisher, Oklahoma, 1914), pp. 119-123, as cited by Botkin.
21. *Weekly Nebraskan*, Milford, Nebraska, August 7, 1885; from the WPA files of the Nebraska State Historical Society.
22. John G. Neihardt, *The River and I* (University of Nebraska Press; Lincoln, 1910), p. 208.
23. From Thomas, p. 34, but also on many tall-tale postcards of the early 20th century.
24. From an anonymous informant in Albion, Nebraska.
25. As above.
26. Thomas, p. 36.
27. From the Bayard, Nebraska, *Transcript*, as reported in the *Omaha World Herald*, July 11, 1971.
28. *Fremont Daily Herald*, August 6, 1895; from the WPA files of the Nebraska State Historical Society.
29. *Fremont Daily Herald*, August 14, 1895; from the WPA files of the Nebraska State Historical Society.
30. *Lyons Mirror*, May 12, 1892; from the WPA files of the Nebraska State Historical Society.
31. From the WPA files of the Nebraska State Historical Society.
32. "Folklore and Western History," *Nebraska History*, July, 1945, p. 15, "from a prize-winning story sent in by Mrs. Alma K. Reck in connection with the Fifth Annual Western Folklore Conference at the University of Denver."
33. From the *Atlantic Monthly*, April, 1959.
34. Hoig, pp. 58-61, from Stewart Edward White's *Arizona Nights* (McClure Company; New York, 1907, as reprinted by Hillman Periodicals, Inc., New York), pp. 165-166.
35. September 21, 1970.
36. *Weekly Burtonian*, August 31, 1887; from the WPA files of the Nebraska State Historical Society. The reference to the *Journal* is not explained.
37. John J. Callison, as quoted by Botkin, pp. 25-26.
38. From an unidentified document in the WPA files of the Nebraska State Historical Society.

39. Anonymous informant in Franklin, Nebraska.
40. From Oscar Henry, whom I miss terribly, Colorado Springs, Colorado.
41. Unidentified Document from the WPA files of the Nebraska State Historical Society, 243.3.
42. *Harpers Weekly*, "Humors of the Day," VIII:368, January 16, 1864, p. 35.
43. These two brief items were collected in Yankton, South Dakota, by Dorothy Shonsey.
44. From Don Messing, Sidney, Nebraska.
45. *Harpers Weekly*, "Things Wise and Otherwise," II:66, April 3, 1858, p. 222.

Sons of the West

1. From an unidentified document in the WPA files of the Nebraska State Historical Society.
2. From the *Lincoln Evening News*, "Walt Mason's Hot Tamales Column," nd.; from the WPA files of the Nebraska State Historical Society. Ezra Savage was acting governor of the State of Nebraska from 1901-1903.
3. *Lincoln Evening News*, "Walt Mason's Hot Tamales Column," October 18, 1901; from the WPA files of the Nebraska State Historical Society.
4. *Weekly Burtonian*, Tekamah, Nebraska, June 8, 1887, apparently from an earlier story in the *Chicago Herald*, no date. From the WPA files of the Nebraska State Historical Society:
   and
   DeWitt Times, January 7, 1886, apparently from an earlier story in the *Chicago Tribune*, no date. From the WPA files of the Nebraska State Historical Society.
5. *Hebron Journal*, September 23, 1875; from the WPA files of the Nebraska State Historical Society.
6. *DeWitt* [sic] *Opposition*, August, 1875; from the WPA files of the Nebraska State Historical Society.
7. *Nebraska Herald*, December 19, 1866; from the WPA files of the Nebraska State Historical Society.
8. As told by Johnny Hahn of Norfolk, Nebraska.
9. *Harpers Weekly*, "Humors of the Day," XI:564, October 19, 1867, p. 663.
10. *Harpers New Monthly Magazine*, XXXIII: CXCI, April, 1866, p. 671.
11. *Harpers Weekly*, "Humors of the Day," X:495, June 23, 1866, p. 395.
12. Collected in Yankton, South Dakota, by Dorothy Shonsey.
13. Mari Sandoz, *Love Song to the Plains* (University of Nebraska Press; Lincoln, 1961), p. 242.

14. *Harpers Weekly*, I:48, November 28, 1857, p. 750.
15. Dee Brown, *The Gentle Tamers* (University of Nebraska Press; Lincoln, 1958), pp. 168-169.
    and
    Harpers Weekly, "Humors of the Day," XI:567, November 9, 1867, p. 711.
16. *Harpers Weekly*, "Wise and Otherwise," I:31, August 1, 1857, p. 494.
17. Told to me by Oscar Henry, Colorado Springs, Colorado.
18. *Tekamah Burtonian*, April 1 [!] 1875; from the WPA files of the Nebraska State Historical Society.
19. *The School Courier*, Kearney, Nebraska, December 15, 1891; from the WPA files of the Nebraska State Historical Society.
20. *Kearney Daily Hub*, July 31, 1909; from the WPA files of the Nebraska State Historical Society.
21. Anonymous informant in Norfolk, Nebraska.
22. *Grand Island Times*, February 4, 1874, courtesy Lynne Ireland.
23. *American Wit and Humor*, Vol. II, (George W. Jacobs and Company; Philadelphia, 1900) p. 197, as cited by Botkin.
24. *Harpers Weekly Magazine*, "Wise and Otherwise," I:13, March 28, 1857.
25. *Harpers Weekly Magazine*, II:88, September 4, 1858, p. 566.
26. *Harpers Weekly Magazine*, II:97, November 6, 1858, p. 718.
27. *Harpers Weekly Magazine*, "Things Wise and Otherwise," II:66, April 3, 1858, p. 222.
28. *Harpers Weekly Magazine*, "Humors of the Day," XII:598, June 13, 1868, p. 379.
29. *Adams County News*, August 9, 1895; from the FWP files of the Nebraska State Historical Society.
30. *Harpers New Monthly Magazine*, XLI:CCXLII, July, 1870, p. 320.
31. As told by Ed Salisbury; from the FWP files of the Wyoming State Historical Society.
32. *Harpers New Monthly Magazine*, "Editor's Drawer," L:CCC, May, 1875, p. 928.
33. *Harpers New Monthly Magazine*, XVII:XCVII, June, 1858, p. 139.
34. *Harpers New Monthly Magazine*, "Editor's Drawer," XXVIII:CLXVII, April, 1864, p. 716.
35. *Harpers New Monthly Magazine*, XXXIX:CCXXXIV, November, 1869, p. 931.
36. An example of this tale appears in *Harpers New Monthly Magazine*, VII:XL, September, 1853, p. 563.
37. *Harpers New Monthly Magazine*, L:CCXCVI, January 1875, pp. 303-304.

38. *Harpers Weekly*, "Things Wise and Otherwise," I:37, September 19, 1857, p. 606.
39. *Harpers Weekly*, "Humors of the Day," XI:557, August 31, 1867, p. 555.
40. Neihardt, *The River and I*, p. 191.
41. *Harpers New Monthly Magazine*, "Editor's Drawer," CCCXXXVI:LXXIII, September, 1886, p. 647.
42. Athearn, p. 73.
43. *Harpers Weekly*, "Things Wise and Otherwise," II:88, September 4, 1858, p. 575.
44. *Flashes and Sparks of Wit and Humor by Our American Humorists* . . . (M. J. Ivers and Co.; New York, 1880), p. 35, as cited by Botkin.
45. From the WPA files of the Wyoming State Historical Society, used here courtesy of James Dow.
46. As told by Abe Abraham in about 1885, from the WPA files of the Wyoming State Historical Society, used here courtesy of James Dow.
47. Phillip Rollins, *The Cowboy, His Characteristics, His Equipment, and His Part in the Development of the West* (reprint edition, Charles Scribner's Sons, New York, 1936), p. 324, as cited by Hoig, p. 127.
48. Athearn, pp. 93-94.
49. *Harpers Weekly*, "Humors of the Day," IV:120, March 31, 1860, p. 195.
50. Athearn, p. 85
51. Athearn, p. 82. Athearn is mistaken in his assumption here that the oyster salesmen were "catering to those of high taste." Oysters were consumed in large quantities at frontier bordellos, especially near mining camps and military posts, because they were believed to increase sexual appetite and capability. Garbage dumps of 19th-century "hog ranches" are distinguished by the preponderance of oyster tins. Thus, quite in contrast with Athearn's suggestion, it is much more likely that the Germans were catering to those of baser, or at any rate more ordinary, tastes.
52. Told of Ethel Dreier from near Ashland, Nebraska.
53. *Harpers New Monthly Magazine*, VIII:XLVIII, May, 1854, p. 709.
54. From the manuscripts of the Federal Writers Project of the WPA for the State of Illinois, Library of Congress Folklore Collection, as cited by Botkin, pp. 316-317.
55. Told by good old Oscar Henry of Colorado Springs, Colorado.

Conclusion

1. Told by an anonymous informant at a meeting of Lincoln Retired Farmers.
2. Told by an anonymous informant in Kearney, Nebraska.